History and Travel Stories
From an Endless Road Trip

Lost In Michigan

Cover Design: Rick Ratell
                Cleaverleaf Design Services
                Midland, MI

Publisher: Etaoin Publishing
                Saginaw, MI
                www.EtaoinPublishing.com

Ordering Information:
Books may be ordered from www.LostinMichigan.net

Printed in the United States of America

ISBN 978-0-9994332-0-1
Category —Michigan History

Dedicated to my wife and children who sat waiting patiently while I get a few pics. "It will only be a few minutes, I promise."

Acknowledgments

Thank you to Anne Reh, for reading through my rough draft and correcting my grammar, it's been a long time since I had an English class and guess I have forgotten a lot of the rules. Hopefully she has kept me from getting in trouble with the grammar police and doing time in grammar jail.

Thank you to Rick Ratell, for designing my cover and the Lost In Michigan logo. His knowledge and skill of graphic design makes me look like I know what I am doing.

I also have to thank my mother for proof reading my book, more than once, I am sure she is getting tired of looking at it, but she never complained.

I definitely have to thank all my loyal followers who read the posts on www.lostinmichigan.net. Your support and kind comments gave me inspiration to write this book.

Introduction

I have always loved traveling around Michigan and like most Michiganders, I would visit popular tourist destinations like Mackinac Island or Tahquamenon Falls. But I have a curious spirit and would always seem to see something along the way that would often create a sense of awe. A few years ago I decided to start finding out about these places of interest and began posting on the Web. Sometimes I would find some place by coincidence while out driving the back roads. Other times I would find an interesting bit of trivia while doing research, either way my curiosity continued to grow.

This book is a culmination of some of my favorite places and stories in the Mitten State. While I have done my best to find accurate information in books, newspapers, and the Internet, some stories are difficult to verify. In some instances the information I find contradicts different sources. Content I find on the Internet I tend to place in low regard unless it is from a trusted website such as an historical society.

Some of the locations highlighted could have an entire book written about them while other places the history and stories have been lost to time, and I could find little information, regardless it still is a fascinating place to me. I hope you enjoy reading the stories and are inspired to go out and explore Michigan for yourself.

The Selected locations in this volume start at the bottom of the state and then work towards the north. Each story is independent of one another and you can read them in any order you wish. I have done my best to give an address that you can use in a GPS to help you find each location. Some places have no address so, I have given a description of where they can be found. Most locations are on public property, but some may be privately owned. Whether they are public or private, they may not be open to visitors or they may be open at scheduled times, but most places can be seen from public roads. I don't trespass and I advise anyone against it. Please be respectful to the places you visit. I hope after reading this book you will take an interest in traveling the back roads of Michigan and seeing what you can find.

Contents

Chapter I Southern Lower Peninsula

Chapter 2 Central Lower Peninsula

Chapter 3 Northern Lower Peninsula

Chapter 4 Upper Peninsula

Chapter 1

Southern Lower Peninsula

Ste Anne De Détroit Church

Location: 1000 Ste. Anne Street, Detroit, MI 48216

While I am traveling around the state, driving through big cites or small towns, I notice the old churches that serve their communities, and I got to wondering, *what is the oldest church in Michigan?* A quick and easy search on Google comes up with Ste. Anne De Detroit. Even though Detroit is not the oldest city in Michigan, (that distinction belongs to Saint Ignace) Detroit is the largest and most prominent city, so it would be no surprise that it would have the oldest church. What is surprising though is how influential the church has been in the history of the state.

Ste. Anne's is the second oldest continuously operating Roman Catholic parish in the United States, with parish records dating back to 1704. Founded on July 26, 1701, Ste. Anne's original church was the first building constructed in Fort Pontchartrain Du Détroit, which later grew into the city of Detroit. The original church was destroyed in 1714 by the people of the fort to keep the Native Americans from using it during a war they were having with them.

The current Ste. Anne's was built in 1886, but it's more than just a beautiful old church, the impact one of it's most prominent priests had on Michigan can still be seen today.

While pastor at Ste. Anne's Father Gabriel Richards, along with Chief Justice Augustus B. Woodward, started a school of higher education in 1817 *Catholepistemiad of Michigania* that became the University of Michigan in 1821. Father Richards owned the first printing press in the young city of Detroit and Published *The Michigan Essay* and *Impartial Observer.* Between 1823 and 1825 Father Richards was Michigan Territory's delegate to the United States Congress. As a delegate, he was instrumental in gaining support for the Territorial Road, which linked Detroit and Chicago.

I think the historic and noble church is not well known to Michiganders because it's not on a heavily traveled road in the heart of downtown Detroit but stands tall in a quiet west-side neighborhood overlooking the houses surrounding it, like a shepherd looking over its flock of sheep. If you are ever the neighborhood behind the old Michigan Central Railroad station, look for the twin steeples rising into the sky and take a drive over to look at the magnificent and historic old Church.

TRIP TIP: The old Detroit firehouse Engine House No. 4 is on the east side of the church on 18th Street and Michigan Central Station is a few blocks to the north.

The Twin Towers

Location: 8433 US-12, Onsted, MI 49265

The Irish Hills area, halfway between Detroit and Chicago, was a popular stage coach stop for the long journey between the two cities. Many immigrants from Ireland came to the area for its rolling hills, giving it its name. As stage coaches gave way to the automobile, motorists would stop in the Irish Hills for a little bit of rest on a long journey. Today it's more of a ghost town of tourist attractions, and the most striking is the Twin Towers. But why would there be two towers? If you think about it, once there is one tower, you should be able see everything from the single structure; there is no need for a second tower next to the first one, unless you are angry about the first tower and build your own tower out of spite.

Thomas Brighton owned half of the tallest hill in the Irish Hills and sold it to the Michigan Observation Company (M.O.C.) They also wanted the other half of the hill but Edward Kelly who owned it declined to sell to them.

In the 1920s the M.O.C. built a tower on their half of the hill. Outraged, Mr. Kelly built a taller tower on his half of the hill to compete with them. Of course the M.O.C. had to respond by raising the height of their tower by adding a second platform and calling it the "Original Irish Hills Towers" Because Mr. Kelly's structure had not been painted, the wood turned a gray color and was called the "Gray Tower," although many of the locals referred to it as the "Spite Tower." Kelly again started to build his tower higher, but the M.O.C. told him that if he did, then they would replace their tower with a steel observation platform that he would not be able to compete with.

Over time, the two built restaurants, golf courses, and other attractions to draw tourists to their tower, but in the long run, they both benefited with the area becoming a popular tourist destination. In the 1950s, Frank Lamping purchased both towers and connected them with a bridge, and in the 1970s, the tops were remodeled with identical platforms. Falling on hard times as tourists found their thrills at other more exciting destinations, the towers closed in 2000. The local township deemed the deteriorating structures unsafe, and the Irish Hills Historical Society removed the upper platforms in 2013 in an effort to stabilize the towers. A Howell, Michigan businessman has recently stepped up to help with an effort to restore the historic old towers, and someday I hope I get the chance to climb up to the top to see the magnificent view of the rolling hills of southern Michigan.

TRIP TIP: The Towers are a few miles east of the Michigan International Speedway.

MichiFact: The Michigan Observation Company also had a tower near Hillsdale on Bundy Hill.

James Scott Castle

Location: 81 Peterboro Street, Detroit, MI 48201

I know it's cliché to take "ruin porn" photos in Detroit, and I prefer to take photos of places that show the beauty of the motor city, but I am also fascinated with castles in Michigan. This old mansion built by James Scott near Wayne State University in Midtown has the look of an old medieval castle in Europe, and I could not resist taking a photo of it. James Scott was a prominent businessman, making his fortune in real estate development in Detroit. When he died in 1870, he gave his fortune to his son, also named James Scott. The younger Scott was not well liked in Detroit society and was a Victorian era "millionaire playboy." In 1897, when he went to purchase the two lots on the corner of Peterboro and Park, the owner of the south lot refused to sell it to him, and out of spite, he built the house three stories tall and without windows facing to the south. The massive three story house blocked out the sun to his neighbor whom he despised.

When he died in 1910, he left the city $200,000 to build a fountain and stipulated that there needed to be a statue of him on it. Because he was not well liked, many of the citizens did not want to build the fountain because of the stipulation and felt he was not worthy of a statue. Some pointed out that he apparently never worked a day in his life and was best known for the time he spent in downtown bars. Eventually it was decided to spend his money and expand Belle Isle and build the fountain that he desired. His request was granted and a statue was placed on the fountain, but on the backside of the fountain, instead of on top where Mr. Scott would have wanted it.

The castle-like home was eventually converted into apartments then suffered from a fire in the 70's and was left abandoned. A developer is in the process of converting it into condominiums. I am looking forward to getting an "after" photo of the restoration to go with this "before" pic from a few years ago.

Trip Tip The Masonic Temple is just a couple of blocks to the south east.

St. Joseph Pier-head Lighthouse

Location: 80 Ridgeway Street, St. Joseph, MI 49085 (this is the address to Tiscornia Park where you can access the north pier to see the lighthouse, Note: there is a small parking fee.)

The lighthouses on Lake Michigan in the southwest part of the state are some of the more unique lighthouses in the country. The St. Joseph pier-head lighthouse towers stand on the end of piers that extend into Lake Michigan and have catwalks that carry electricity to power the light and also allow the light keeper to walk out to the light to maintain it while the pounding waves crash against the side of the pier. The St. Joseph Lighthouse is one of the more popular lighthouses in the Mitten State and is a favorite location to watch a dramatic Lake Michigan sunset. In the winter months the lighthouse can get consumed by ice from the waves exploding over it during the unforgiving winter storms. When I visited on a blustery February day the light was not completely engulfed by ice, but the pier was covered in ice and snow which made for a challenging walk to the end of it. It was a little treacherous but not impossible to walk on. If you have some ice spikes to slip on over your boots, that would be helpful in getting a grip on the slippery surface. On the day I was there in February, some hearty fishermen were casting their lines off the side of the pier in hopes that they would land a "big one." I think they were looking at me thinking I was a crazy photographer; and, all the while, I was thinking they were crazy fishermen, but we must all pursue our happiness.

The first lighthouse in St. Joesph was erected in 1832 on the shoreline and was the second lighthouse constructed on Lake Michigan. Two piers were extended out into the lake in 1870 to protect the ships entering the St. Joseph River, and a beacon was placed at the pier-head. In the early 1900s, the war department expanded the piers, and in 1907, the current lighthouse was built. It consisted of two lights known as "Range Lights" that sailors would align to ensure that they were entering straight into the channel. A catwalk was also constructed, allowing the lighthouse keepers to access the light during severe storms. In 2008, the United States Coast Guard decided the lighthouse was no longer necessary for navigation and gave it to the city of St. Joseph. The Lighthouse Forever Fund raised money to restore the landmark structure making it one of the most popular destinations for lighthouse lovers.

Trip Tip: The best way to access the pier is to go to Tiscornia Park. It's a little tricky to find, but make sure you take the fork in the road to the right onto Marina Drive from Upton Drive.

Michi-Fact: The city was originally named Newburyport when it was plated in 1829, but the name was changed to St. Joseph in 1832 for the river it is on, which was named by French Missionaries.

The Haunted Eloise Asylum

Location: 30712 Michigan Avenue
Westland, MI 48185

Some say that the Eloise Asylum, in Westland on Michigan Ave., is one of Michigan's most haunted places. I am not sure about that claim, but it was at one time Michigan's largest hospital and sanitarium. Although most of it is gone, what remains is peculiar and hauntingly beautiful which makes it easy to wonder about it's past and speculate if it is truly haunted.

The location where the old buildings now stand began in 1939 when a log cabin known as the Black Horse Tavern and its property were converted into a poorhouse. Thirty five of the overcrowded tenants in Hamtramck at the Wayne County poorhouse that provided housing for the needy were transferred to the newly constructed buildings. For years it was known as the Wayne County Poorhouse until a post office was opened in 1894 and named after Eloise Dickerson Davock, the daughter of Detroit's postmaster.

In 1913 there were three divisions: The Eloise Hospital (Mental Hospital), the Eloise Infirmary (Poorhouse) and the Eloise Sanitarium (T.B. Hospital). Over the years the complex continued to grow with about 10,000 residents at its peak during the Great Depression. It had its own police and fire department, railroad and trolley stations, bakery, amusement hall, laundries, and a powerhouse for electricity. It also had many farm buildings, including a dairy herd and dairy barns, a pig farm, a root cellar, a tobacco curing building, and employee housing.

Dr. Albarran, working at Eloise, was one of the first (if not the first) doctor to use X-rays and patients came from Detroit and other communities to be able to "see" inside their body. It also housed the first kidney dialysis unit in the State of Michigan and was a pioneer in the field of Music Therapy.

The other parts of Eloise that remain are the cemeteries and with a complex that had about 10,000 people living there, death was a regular occurrence. There were a few different locations that the bodies of the patients and residents of the poorhouse were buried. One of the cemeteries is about a mile to the south down Henry Ruff road and is nothing more than a field with small stone markers engraved with only a number for the body buried below. It seems rather cruel and inhumane that a person is remembered as a number, and not even a name was placed on the marker. The cemeteries were used up until 1948; after that, a law was enacted to use the bodies as cadavers for medical training. (I was not able to get a photo of the markers since the cemetery is fenced off and says "No Trespassing", and I really don't want to go to jail.)

The farm operations ceased in 1958, and some of the large psychiatric buildings were vacated in 1973. The psychiatric division started closing in 1977 when the State of Michigan took over the psychiatric division. The general hospital closed in 1984. Many of the buildings are gone and some of the property has been redeveloped into a golf course and condominiums. There is a Michigan Historical Marker near the parking lot, and currently the main building is up for sale. The hospital was used as a filming location for the 2017 horror movie *Eloise* directed by Robert Legato. It was a fictional movie based on the hospital and it will add to the rumors of the old building being haunted.

Trip Tip: Heading east on Michigan Avenue will take you to the Henry Ford Museum, and traveling west will take you to Ypsilanti and Ann Arbor.

Climax Post Office and R.F.D.

Location: 107 N Main Street, Climax, MI 49034

Delivering packages with drones seems really far fetched, but a century ago, delivering mail to everyone in the united states seemed like an impossible task. Many small rural towns had a post office that was in a local general store, saloon, or inn. The farmers or ranchers would come into town and pick up their mail. In 1893, legislation was passed in the United State congress that required the post office to implement rural free delivery (R.F.D). On December 3, 1896, the post office in the town of Climax, between Battle Creek and Kalamazoo, was the first to start an R.F.D. route in Michigan. The letter carriers delivered the mail by bicycle or horse and buggy to the surrounding citizens. The old stone post office in Climax, which is now a library, still stands in the heart of downtown Climax.

The local businesses that contained the post offices were not too fond of the new delivery system since people did not have to pick up their mail, and possibly utilize this stop to purchase something at their business while they were in town. It's strangely similar to the online versus brick and mortar store competition. Who knows in another hundred years there may be something new, some sort of outer space colony delivery system, and they will think what we do now was old fashioned.

The community was so proud of their RFD route that they built a magnificent stone monument in the center of the main intersections with field stones collected from each of the farms on the route. After World War II, the monument was a hazard to traffic so it was moved to a nearby park in town.

Michi-Fact: The town of Climax got its name in 1838 when it was named Climax Prairie when the first settlers determined it was the "climax" in their search for a place to settle.

Hecker Castle on Woodward

Location: 5510 Woodward Avenue Detroit, MI 48201

There are five main roads that radiate out from the center of downtown Detroit. Among the five, it's Woodward Avenue that runs North from the Motor City to Pontiac. Woodward Ave, named for judge Augustus B. Woodward, was the first mile of paved highway in the country, and named by author Robert Genat as the "Father Road," in his book about the historic highway. There are many beautiful and historic churches, homes, and buildings on Woodward Ave

16

including the Detroit Institute of Arts, but its the French Renaissance styled castle that captures my attention because it looks like it belongs in the French countryside.

The castle was the home of railroad and ship-building baron Col. Frank J. Hecker. In 1888, Hecker hired architect Louis Kamper and began constructing on the mansion on Woodward Avenue. The massive 21,000 square feet home was used by Hecker to host elaborate parties where he entertained luminaries such as presidents William McKinley and Rutherford B. Hayes.

The interior has 49 rooms, including a large oak-paneled hall designed for large parties, an oval dining room done in mahogany, a lobby finished in English oak, and a white and gold music room. There are more than a dozen fire places to heat the grand old castle.

The law firm of Charfoos & Christensen purchased the mansion in 1991 for $660,000 and invested $1.6 million into renovating the building. The firm used the former residence as their offices until 2014 when Wayne State University purchased the majestic castle for use by the Alumni Relations department. Next time you are traveling down Woodward, I hope you will keep a look out for one of the most spectacular castles in Michigan.

Photo Tip Cloudy days are a good day to take photographs of buildings in big cities because you don't have to worry about the direction of the sun or shadows from other buildings.

The Historic Ypsilanti Water Tower

Location: Intersection of North Summit and Washtenaw Avenue, Ypsilanti, MI 48197

Traveling into Ypsilanti from US 23, east on Washtenaw Ave., it's hard to miss the giant stone water tower. The historical stone structure has a domed roof that looks like a big ... (I better not say it, but you can imagine what some people say it looks like).

Constructed in 1890, the water tower sits atop the tallest hill in Ypsilanti and is 147 feet tall and 85 foot diameter at the base with forty inch thick walls to support the 250,000 gallon steel tank. During construction of the tower, stone crosses were placed in the stonework as a way to protect the workers. One cross is visible over the front door. To pay for the tower, the city charged residents $5 for a faucet and $2 for a private bath, and for each cow, they were charged $1. People who did not pay their water bill had to pay a $50 fine and spend 90 days in jail. The water tower was the only one to provide water in Ypsilanti until another one was built in 1956.

The town of Ypsilanti was named after Demetrios Ypsilantis, a hero in the Greek War of Independence. A marble bust of him is on display in front of the water tower along with the American flag and the Greek Flag. Getting back to what the tower looks like, it was voted as the most phallic building in the United States. Writer Jonathan Ames claimed that the Williamsburg Bank Building in Brooklyn, New York was the world's most phallic building. In 2003, *Cabinet Magazine* had a contest for the most phallic building. With several entries from around the country, they picked the Ypsilanti water tower as the winner.

Trip Tip: When you're in Ypsilanti, keep heading down Washtenaw Road toward the river to Depot Town to the old historic part of Ypsilanti for some local bars and restaurants.

Michi Fact: Elija McCoy invented the self lubricator for trains in his Ypsilanti shop, and it's believed the phrase "The Real McCoy" came from here.

The Old State Prison in Jackson

Location: 100 Armory Court. Jackson 49202

On my first trip to Jackson, I wanted to see the old prison. I did not write down the address, and figured I would find it since it has to be a large complex and not that hard to miss. I came into Jackson from the north, down M-106, which turns into Cooper Street and goes past the east side of the prison. There were some buildings and a parking lot next to the old stone wall, and somehow I went right past it. The wall was so large that I did not realize it was part of the prison. I guess it just goes to show that sometimes what you are looking for is actually right in front of you and you didn't even know it. It really is a large wall surrounding the complex. It's one of those places you have to visit because it's extremely difficult to show just how large it is in a photograph.

The first state prison opened in 1838 near Jackson, and started with a temporary wooden prison. In 1839, the first thirty-five prisoners were received. It started with three log cabins and walls built with huge wide logs, almost like a fur traders post. Seven of the original thirty-five prisoners escaped over the walls. Then two years after it opened, on a foggy night June 1, 1840, ten of the eighty-five inmates dug their way out of the cabins and escaped. The fugitives terrorized the community, robbing banks and becoming known as the Jackson Robber Gang. It took two years to ultimately capture the final eight escapees. In 1861, the west end of the prison complex was completed to house prisoners of the Civil War, and it was quickly overcrowded.

John Morris, the warden from 1870 to 1875, was prosecuted for his brutality to prisoners. Morris once had a prisoner whipped sixty-three times. Another, who had suffered an injury to an arm during the Civil War was tied against a wall with wet leather bands at the wrists and ankles. By the time the bands had dried and the man was untied, his arm was so severely injured it had to be amputated. The assistant warden, thirty-three inmates, firefighters, doctors and seemingly anyone else involved in prison life testified at his trial. Morris had a wonderful demeanor to the outside world, but inside the prison, he became a monster.

Beginning in the 1880s under Warden H. F. Hatch, a greater emphasis was placed on education and rehabilitation of prisoners. Female prisoners were at the Michigan State Prison with the men until 1882. Sarah Havilland poisoned her own children because she couldn't feed them. Yet inside the prison she became the much beloved caregiver to the warden's children, who at the time lived on site. By 1882, it was the largest walled prison in the world and a quarter of the size of Jackson in terms of population. On September 1, 1912, a riot that was described by many as the "worst riot in the prison's history" began. The first sign of trouble was when inmates starting throwing plates against the walls of the dining halls. Many fights followed after this and the riot lasted for six days. On the sixth day, the ninety or so inmates who were leading the riot were beaten. The riot eventually came to an end, but not until after the governor had called in the National Guard.

In 1928, construction of a new prison north of Jackson began and the inmates were moved to the new facility. The old prison was closed in 1934, and at the time there were 3,840 Despite the many additional cell blocks that were added through the years, there were too many prisoners for the facility to handle.

Trip Tip: If you would like a guided tour of the old prison visit www.historicprisontours.com

The Heart of Rock and Roll in Kalamazoo

Location: 225 Parsons Street in Kalamazoo 49007

When I went to look for the old Gibson guitar factory in Kalamazoo, I started thinking I was actually lost. I was driving through an old neighborhood past a school, houses, and a church and started thinking that I was in the wrong place; but then I came upon the old factory-like a temple of music in an old city.

24

There would not be rock 'n' roll without an electric guitar; and when it comes to guitars, there is nothing more iconic than Gibson. The company started out when Orville Gibson patented a mandolin in 1902. With the success of the mandolins, the company began building acoustic guitars. Then history was made in 1950 when Les Paul who was hired by the company as a consultant. Shortly after Gibson created the Les Paul line of electric guitars. In the mid 1980s the company left Kalamazoo and moved to Nashville, but the proud Michiganders who worked in the factory stayed to create the Heritage Guitar Corporation and they continue making would class guitars. The factory is an interesting-looking building with its front entrance that gives the appearance of a vestibule on an old church, which makes the building look like a temple to the rock gods. The old smokestack with GIBSON laid out in tiles stands along the back of the plant. It was scheduled to be demolished, but the owners have made the decision to rebuild the iconic smokestack and are in the process of a 12 million dollar renovation of the building with talk of creating a restaurant or bar inside it.

Trip Tip Heritage Guitar Inc. offer tours of the factory. You can find out more at www.heritageguitar.com/tour/

MichiFact: The name Kalamazoo is from the Native American word *kikalamazoo* meaning mirage or reflecting river.

Downtown Ann Arbor

Location: The corner of Main Street and Liberty

If you're looking for a vibrant downtown to go hang out in, you can't go wrong with Ann Arbor. It's definitely a college town with the University of Michigan located in the city, but it's also a great tourist destination. It has a plethora of fascinating and fun places to explore and to shop at, from coffee houses, book stores, art galleries and boutiques, there is plenty to see and do.

While you are there you can get a hamburger at the world famous Crazy Jim's Blimpy Burger at 304 S. Ashley St. It was featured on *Diners, Drive-Inns and Dives* with Guy Fieri, along with other shows for foodies. Just make sure you follow the rules posted on the wall when ordering or they won't be to happy with you holding up the line.

One thing I have learned, when making a trip to Ann Arbor in the fall: be sure to check the football schedule for U of M and make sure there is not a home game, otherwise it's a zoo, a fun zoo of Wolverine fans, but it's really crowded. The summer or holiday weekends are also a great time to go site seeing, that's when most of the students are at home. Even if you are a Michigan State Spartan, I think it makes for a fun day trip exploring downtown Ann Arbor. And yes, Wolverines should check out East Lansing, but that's for the next book.

Trip Tip I think the easiest place to find a parking spot downtown is in the Fourth and William Street parking structure at 115 E William St. Ann Arbor, MI 48104

Michi Fact the name Ann Arbor comes from the arbors (natural groves) in the area when the first two settlers came to the region in 1823. John Allen and Walker Rumsey named the town after their wives both named Ann.

Felt Mansion

Location: 6597 138th Avenue Holland, MI 49423

Some say that the Felt Mansion is haunted, and when I made the trip out to see it in late winter on a gloomy day, it sure felt (no pun intended) spooky. It seemed like it was built in the middle of nowhere after I drove through the woods and grasslands to get to it. The house is isolated from civilization, but I guess that would be the point if you wanted a home to escape the hustle and bustle of the big city.

The construction of Felt Mansion was completed in 1928 as a summer retreat for Dorr Eugene Felt and his family. He was a wealthy businessman from Chicago and he made his fortune, inventing and manufacturing the Comptometer, a mechanical calculator businesses used for book keeping. Mr. Felt fell in love with the Lake Michigan shoreline and purchased hundreds of acres near Holland, calling it Shore Acres Farm. The mansion is over twelve hundred square feet with 25 rooms. It has a large third floor ballroom to entertain guests. Unfortunately six weeks after the family moved into the grand home, Mr Felt's wife Agnes died and it was only a year and a half later Dorr Felt, himself, passed away and joined his wife. The grand old home remained in the Felt family for several years.

After World War II, electronic calculators began replacing the mechanical calculators that Dorr Felt had so ingeniously created. In 1949, the family auctioned off the the contents of the mansion and sold it to The St. Augustine Seminary, a Catholic prep school. They used the carriage house for the school and the mansion for housing. The State of Michigan purchased the property and home in the 1970s converting it to offices for the State Police and erected a minimum security prison on the site. When the State no longer needed the old mansion in the 1990s they sold it to Laketown Township, the township that the estate is located in, for one dollar. The State stipulated that it always be available to the public, and not be sold to private hands.

The Mansion was restored in early 2000 and is used for weddings, receptions, and other public events.

Over the years the sudden death of Agnes Felt has fueled rumors of the old house being haunted. It is believed Agnes's and her husband's spirits roam the mansion; since they had so little time to enjoy it, they reside there in the afterlife. There is also a myth that strange children with large bulbous heads known as "mellonheads" roam the woods surrounding the estate. As the story goes, there was an old hospital nearby where a doctor performed experiments on the children. Some of the children escaped and still lurk among the trees plotting revenge on the doctor. The local historical society has said that there was never any hospital nearby, but the myth has been perpetuated for generations.

Despite the hauntings, and so-called *mellonheads* it is a beautiful mansion and accessible to the public. You can find out more at their website www.feltmansion.org

Trip Tip: Shore Acres Township Park is located next to the mansion and has miles of hiking trails and a disc golf course. Right down the road is Saugatuck Dunes State Park with two and a half miles of shoreline on Lake Michigan and miles of trails for hiking and bird watching.

Livingstone Memorial Light

Location: eastern tip of Belle Isle

There are several lighthouses and navigational lights in Michigan, about a 150 of them if you didn't already know. The Livingston Memorial Light is one of the most unique not only in Michigan but in the United States. It's one of only three lights erected as a memorial in Michigan, and the only navigational light constructed of marble in the country. William Livingston was a prominent businessman in

Detroit, and served as president of the Lake Carriers Association. He was instrumental in having the government expand the Soo locks, and deepening and widening the channel in the St Mary's river. He also worked on the project, building a waterway for down-bound ships in the lower Detroit River. The channel opened in 1908, and named the Livingstone Channel in his honor. During the early 1900s, more ships and tonnage passed by Detroit than through either the Suez or Panama canals. After his death in 1925, as a tribute to Livingston, the city of Detroit donated the property on Belle Isle. Funds were raised by the Lakes Carriers Association to build the $100,000 tower designed by famed Detroit architect Albert Kahn. The art deco style tower is made of white Georgian marble, and has a light that can be seen for 16 miles on Lake St. Clair. There was another lighthouse on the island before the memorial light was built. The Belle Isle lighthouse was constructed in 1881 in the same location where the Coast Guard station resides on Belle Isle. Keeper Louis Fetes lived at the lighthouse for nearly 40 years. He and his wife raised their six children on the island. In 1930 the light was automated, and by the 40s the old forgotten lighthouse began to decay, and the coast guard demolished it.

Trip Tip: Be sure to visit the Belle Isle Aquarium and the Anna Scripps Whitcomb Conservatory while you are there. Also remember the island is a State Park and a fee or Recreation Passport on you plates is required for entry.

Rattle Run Church Murder

Location: The corner of Rattle Run Road and Gratiot Road in St Clair county (the town and the church are no longer there)

The long forgotten town of Rattle Run, and the church that the townsfolk once worshiped inside has been gone for a long time. Most Michiganders have forgotten about it, but one of Michigan's most gruesome murders took place in the old church. The town, named after the nearby rattling rapids of Columbus Creek, was located in Columbia Township southwest of Port Huron. In January of 1909, the church caretaker made a shocking discovery of blood in the snow. When he looked inside the the church, it was in complete disarray, and there was blood splattered everywhere. He contacted Sheriff Waggensell in Port Huron. Upon investigating the scene, human body parts were found in the wood stove used to heat the church. The minister at the church, Rev. John Haviland Carmichael was nowhere to be found. A few days after the murder, a man by the name of John Elder showed up in the town of Carthage, Illinois. For a man traveling, he did not carry any baggage, and rented a room at a boarding house run by Mrs. Hughes. He told her he was a cabinet maker passing through town. Mr. Elder was acting very strangely, and when Mrs. Hughes gave him dinner, he said he was fasting and would not eat anything. The next morning she made him a large breakfast figuring he would be hungry. Instead of eating, he simply gathered what little he had, paid his bill, and said he was leaving for a job twelve miles away. A few moments later, she heard a noise in the shed and was afraid to look for herself. She called a neighbor, but they were not home. Then, a mailman walked by, and when he looked in the shed he found Mr. Elder lying on the floor with blood gushing out of his neck and a knife in his hands. He was still alive, but died shortly after. The local sheriff in Carthage found two letters; one addressed to Mrs. Carmichael in Rattle Run and the other to Sheriff Waggensell in Port Huron. Both letters were almost identical, and were published in several newspapers across the country.

To Mr. Waggensell (Sheriff of St. Clair County)

Port Huron, Mich.

dated Jan. 9, 1909

Carthage, Illinois,

Honored Sir: I write this letter to explain in connection with a Columbus Creek tragedy. I am guilty only because I am a coward. The man (Amos Gideon Browning) had such a hypnotic influence over me that I felt that something must be done. I felt greatly ashamed that a man said to be short minded should be able to compel me to yield to his will.

At first he said:" It's all right, elder, don't be afraid".
Then he began to talk about how we two could get rich.
Three times he came to the rear of my barn and talked
to me. Twice he was at the river when I went to water
my stock, and each time I felt that he was doing
something he was proud of.

Once when I was going out to Columbus he was on the
pike, near the pink school-house, when I overtook him,
he asked to ride, which I could not refuse. He asked me
if ever I had driven the pike to Port Huron, to which I
answered no. Then he said: 'Come on, lets drive up to
Port Huron,' which I resented, but he kept on until he
persuaded me to go.

He got out and stood at the corner while I went to the
barn with the rig. Then later we had been at the
restaurant, for which he paid. He gave me a half dollar
and said he wanted me to go there and buy a small
hatchet for his boy to play with. I began to tell him to
go and do his own buying, he set his eyes upon me with
the queerest sort of a look, something like a look of a
snake's eye.

All the while I felt his influence tighten on my mind, so
I went. Intending to go into the store and out the back
way to get the horse and rush off for home. When I
turned to close the door he stood looking upon me
through the window and I just bought the hatchet and
came out again, but by that time he had disappeared, I
went into the barn, got my rig, and started for home,

when as I made the turn onto Military street he was at the corner to get in.

He rode as far as South Park, where he got out to take the car, and he took the hatchet with him and said nothing, nor did I think anything at the time about it.

When at the depot at Adair, he came out of the house and compelled me to walk the rails. All the while I felt as small as a bantam chicken. When he arranged with me about the wedding he wanted, he would go to Port Huron and get the license and meet me on the road between that place and the church.

I thought that he really meant to get married when he engaged my services, but when we met in the road and he was alone I began to feel uneasy, but he said it was all right, the others would come in a carriage. When we went into the church I wanted to light a lamp, to which he dissented, saying; "No, elder, no light unless they should come". But, presently, he said "maybe we better have a little fire". So I went out and passed wood to him through the window.

When I had put in what I thought would be enough, he said: "now, elder, the moonlight is shining right on the front-door, and if you go around there to come in some one may see you. Just pile up some wood here and come in through this window.' I brought a few sticks and laid them across each other, from the top of which he helped me into the building. he let the window nearly down again and we kept looking out through the opening to see if the others came down the state road.

He took a big hearty laugh and said: 'There ain't no use looking, for there ain't going to be no wedding.' He was sitting where a gleam of light shone on his face and his eyes were so brilliant that I was thrilled through and through. Queerest sort of feeling. I asked him why, then, he had made the present arrangement, when he said:

Well, elder, I just wanted to have a little fun. You consider yourself an educated man and look down on a poor ignorant fellow like me, and I just thought I would show you. I knowed if I could handle you I could handle other men and make a big thing out of it. Now if I say, raise your hand, up she goes. See, that is no dream, and I felt my hand raising without any effort whatever on my part.

Then he said: If I say let down your hand. down it goes.' and I felt it going down in. a singular manner. By this time I was so alarmed that I was in a cold sweat. I then leaned over to see if any one might be on the road, when he began to laugh again, and I saw that he was holding a weapon up his sleeve. Instantly I made a grab for it and got the hatchet from him and asked what he meant to do with that, and he said: "I will show you. and from his overcoat pocket he drew out a knife with each hand.

He came at me striking with both hands. I backed across the church, down the side aisle and across the front, but I did not dare to turn about to the front door. Then I threw the hatchet and struck him and he fell. I then turned to open the door, when he grabbed me by the leg and threw me down where my hand came upon the hatchet.

There was a desperate struggle in which I used the hatchet until he lay quiet and still. I cannot recall all that happened after that. I was wild to dispose of the body. I was in a horrible terror, I began pulling off his garments that I might drag the body away somewhere and hide it. When he woke up and grabbed me again. Then for a while I used that hatchet until I was sure he was dead.

I waited until I saw the fire was hot enough to make a stove pipe red nearly to the elbow I grabbed him and dragged him down there and began cutting him to pieces, putting in each piece as it was dismembered. Then I began to put the garments into the stove. Then I saw that my clothing was cut and bloody while some of his was yet whole and I exchanged them and then took all the bloody clothes and piled them in along with the body. My big coat hid my torn and bloody clothes until I got to Chicago, where I purchased others.

I am tired of trying to hide. Though I have succeeded in eluding the detectives so far. If you get this and I am yet alive, come and get me. I shall be not far from Carthage, Illinois.

Rev. W. J. Carmichael

Chapter 2
Central Lower Peninsula

Curwood Castle

Location: 224 Curwood Castle Dive, Owosso, MI 48867

Many years ago I traveled to Lansing from my hometown of Saginaw and I took the "back way" down M52 through Owosso. I noticed out of the corner of my eye a large yellowish-orange castle a block east of M52 and had to check it out. When you hear the name of Steven King or J.K. Rowling right away most people know them as famous authors. In the early 1900s James Oliver Curwood was a famous author and just like writers today his books were made into movies. The 1988 movie *The Bear* was based on his novel *The Grizzly King* and the Movie *The Trail Beyond* staring John Wayne was based on his novel *The Wolf Hunters.* I have always admired him, not only for his writing, but because he chose to build his own castle for a writing studio instead of constructing a plain ordinary building.

James Oliver Curwood was born in Owosso on June 12, 1878, and lived there most of his life. Writing and a love of nature were his boyhood interests, and by 1908 Curwood was earning his living as a novelist. Most of his stories were adventure tales set in the Canadian north, where the author spent much of his time. During the 1920s his books were among the most popular in North America, and many were made into early black and white motion picture movies.

The French chateau castle on the banks of the Shiawassee River was built in 1922, where he spent his days in the tower writing. Curwood was an active conservationist, and in 1926, he was appointed to the Michigan Conservation Commission. He died at his home not far from the castle on Williams Street on August 13, 1927. After he died, the Castle was given to the city of Owosso. It has served in various capacities over the years and is now a museum operated by the city, and is open to the public.

Every Summer, the Curwood Festival takes place at the magnificent old castle to celebrate the life and works of James Oliver Curwood.

Michi Fact:: Mount Curwood, near L'Anse with an elevation of 1,978 feet is the second highest point in the state of Michigan. Named in honor of James Oliver Curwood it was designated as Michigan's highest point until a resurvey in 1982 with modern technology determined that nearby Mount Arvon is actually 1,979 feet high, one foot taller than Mount Curwood.

Trip Tip: there are several historic homes in Owosso in the neighborhood just north of downtown.

Bruce Mansion

Location: 5977 Van Dyke
Brown City, MI 48416

It would not be strange to see a large three-story second empire-style mansion in a large Michigan city. Finding one in northern Lapeer county in the middle of farm land is peculiar. It's difficult to miss this hauntingly beautiful house painted light green on M-53 Near Brown City, in Burnside Township.

The massive, ornate mansion was built in 1876 by John G. Bruce. He owned the Bruce and Webster General Merchants with his brother-in-law. Burnside Township was originally Allison Township, but the name was changed in 1866 to honor Ambrose E. Burnside, a union general in the Civil War. John G. Bruce was the postmaster for 16 years in Burnside. Most of the town was destroyed by a fire in 1881, but the mansion and general store were spared from the flames. In 1894 Bruce lost the general store to a fire, and rebuilt it with a brick building.

Bruce eventually sold the home to Cynthia Smith who died in the house from a fever in 1921. Cynthia's son sold the house, and it changed owners a few times. It was eventually purchased by John Walker in 1926. Rumor has it, he was driving his automobile when he hit a pedestrian. Terrified at what he had done, he took the body back to the mansion and buried it somewhere on the estate. Some say the ghost of the victim, others say guilt, caused Walker to lose his fortune and he hanged himself in the mansion's tower. It is said to be haunted; I am not sure about that, but it is a beautiful old house. It's kind of spooky with the ghostly light green paint, and it seems like an odd location for such an nonvenomous mansion that would expect to be in a large city and not standing among the farm fields.

The house is privately owned, but they do offer paranormal investigation tours: You can find out more on their website www.mihaunted.com

House of Seven Gables

Location: 7995 Pioneer Drive
Port Austin, MI 48467

At the tip of the thumb, south of Grindstone City, on M-23, there is a sign for Huron City Museum. It's not your ordinary museum with a building and a collection of artifacts inside;

instead, the buildings themselves are the collection of artifacts.

Among the buildings that make up the collection is The House of Seven Gables, a beautifully preserved Victorian home that sits on a bluff overlooking Lake Huron. It was named by William Lyon Phelps for the house of the same name in the Hawthorne novel. This is the third house built on this site. The great forest fires of 1871 and 1881 that annihilated the timber in the Thumb destroyed the two houses built before this one.

Annabel Hubbard decorated Seven Gables in 1886 for her father Langdon Hubbard. After her marriage to William Lyon Phelps, Annabel added "modern" bathrooms and updated several rooms in the early 1900s. The furniture inside is original to the house, and major portions of the house still have the original 1886 decorations.

Before Langdon Hubbard came to Huron City, Theodore Luce built a water powered sawmill on Willow Creek in 1837. A fellow from Port Huron by the name of Mr. Brakeman (somehow his first name was lost to history) purchased the old sawmill in 1852, and the area became known as Brakeman's Creek. Four years later in 1854 is when Langdon Hubbard purchased the mill from Mr. Brakeman. In 1856, the town was given a post office by the name of Willow Creek. The post office was closed seven months later in November of 1856. A few months later, it was opened again but with the new name of Huron City. Langdon was a smart businessman and the town thrived and even survived after being destroyed by the devastating fires of 1871 and 1881. The post office closed in 1905 but the town continued on. Now, the city is an historic landmark with the buildings maintained by the William Lyon Phelps Foundation. The buildings on the property constitute the Huron City Museums. If you are ever near the tip of the thumb, be sure to check out the historic town with its many buildings including the House of Seven Gables, a general store, and a church. The museum is open on weekends for tours and you can find more info on their website at www.huroncitymuseums.org

Trip Tip: Point Aux Barques lighthouse is just a few miles to the south of Huron City.

Hell's Half Mile in Bay City

Location: Water Street, Downtown Bay City

Downtown Bay City is a favorite destination for Michiganders to go "antiquing" in the shops along Water Street. It's also an fine place to get something to eat in a restaurant or a cup of joe in a coffee shop. About a century and a half ago, this now peaceful downtown full of tourists was something totally opposite.

In the late 1800s, after the lumbering season was done, lumberjacks and shanty boys would head out of the woods and into town. Their pockets were filled with pay that they just had received for a season of hard work harvesting timber in the northern woods of Michigan. Bay City was one of the first places the lumberjacks came to spend their money on their favorite vice such as alcohol, gambling, and prostitutes. Water Street, along the Saginaw River, was there waiting for them with a plethora of businesses looking to separate the lumberjack from his hard-earned money. After months in the woods, they were happy to spend money at the saloons, dance halls, and brothels, drinking and gambling in the downtown blocks on water street. The owners of the saloons would have the pretty waitresses standing at the door to attract the men to their establishment, hopefully, before they had the chance to visit one of their competitors.

The area was known for large drunken brawls, giving it the nickname "Hell's Half Mile". The smart saloon keeper would have a gang of "professional fighters" to keep the peace in their establishment. There were tunnels and catacombs that ran under the city streets and buildings, allowing passage from saloons and brothels, without being seen, or maybe even to drag a dead body out to hide elsewhere. The police did not have the force to control the throng of rowdy lumberjacks, who, after a few weeks, would run out of money and have their desires fulfilled. Finally, the town would get back to a calmer sense of normal.

It's believed that Paul Bunyan was based the real-life lumberjack. Fabian "Saginaw Joe" Fournier was a giant of a man and camp boss in the Saginaw Valley. He was murdered on the docks in Downtown Bay City in 1875. The book *Paul Bunyan: How A Terrible Timber Feller Became A Legend* written by D. Laurence Rogers explores the link between Fournier and Paul Bunyan.

Michi Fact: The first person to go over Niagara Falls in a barrel and survive was a 63 year-old dance instructor from Bay City, Annie Edson Taylor on October 24, 1901.

The Death of the Sparling Men in Tyre

Above: The old abandoned grain elevator in Tyre

Location: Tyre is in the center of the thumb, south of Ubly, on Tyre Road between, Huron Line Road and Bay City Forestville Road.

Doctors have always been a well- respected part of a community and the person we turn to when we need help. It was a family and their mysterious deaths after being treated by a doctor that became one of Michigan's most historic criminal cases.

John Wesley Sparling and his family lived on their farm near the village of Tyre, named after the Biblical place of Tyre because of its stony terrain. Fifty three year old John and his wife Carrie had four sons and a daughter, who was married and lived with her husband. On a hot summer day in 1909, John Wesley Sparling collapsed while clutching his stomach. His oldest son Peter rode into town to get Dr. Robert A. MacGregor, who diagnosed a kidney ailment. A short time later John Wesley died from whatever had caused his health problems.

About a year later, 25-year-old Peter staggered from a field while gathering hay and died five days later. After the deaths of John and Peter, Dr. McGregor advised John's wife Carrie to take out life insurance policies on her remaining two sons. Albert, the second oldest Sparling, became ill in church the following year after Peter died. Both of John's other sons had died with similar symptoms as their father. On August 4, 1911, the same symptoms arose on John's son Scyrel but this time a different doctor treated him. Dr. Conboy suspected poisoning and reported it to local authorities. Scyrel grew worse and died August 14, 1911 leaving only the youngest son Raymond alive.

The prosecutor ordered the examination of Scyrel's organs and had them sent to the University of Michigan which reported finding arsenic. The body of Albert was exhumed and examined. The University of Michigan declared it was death by arsenic poisoning. Dr. MacGregor was arrested, and tried for the murders of the four men in a trial which gained national attention. The prosecutor presented a case that John Wesley Sparling's wife, Carrie, was having an affair with the doctor, and that he had her take out life insurance policies on her children who were strong and healthy at the time. Dr. MacGregor was found guilty of murder in the first degree and sentenced to life in prison. Carrie Sparling's charges against her were dropped due to insufficient evidence.

After Michigan Governor Nathan Ferris received an appeal on MacGregor's behalf, he had the case re-investigated. The results of the re-investigation were not made public, so it is not known what facts it established. Nevertheless, in 1916, the governor issued MacGregor a full and unconditional pardon, and the governor took the unusual step of having MacGregor brought to the state capital in Lansing where he handed him the pardon, personally. In his statement the Governor said, "I am firmly convinced that Dr. MacGregor is absolutely innocent of the crime for which he was convicted." The governor shortly thereafter appointed MacGregor as the official state doctor to the Jackson State Prison where he had just been an inmate, again without explanation. MacGregor died in 1928.

Author and relative of the Sparling family Jacki Howard has written a book about the murders called *The Thumb Pointed Fingers.* You can find out more on the website www.dyingsparlings.com.

Trip Tip: The Sanilac Petroglyphs Historic State Park is a few miles to the west. It contains Michigan's only known rock carvings by Native Americans.

The Cat Lady House in Saginaw

Location: 633 Washington Ave. Saginaw, MI 48601

One of the most well-known houses according to the people who live in Saginaw, has to be the "Cat Lady's House" on Washington Ave. near the railroad tracks just south of downtown Saginaw. There was an eccentric woman who lived there, and it was rumored that she had a lion or tiger for a pet, but actually it was a leopard and her name was Rosemary. Long before she and her pet leopard Chichu lived in the old house, it was built by one of Saginaw's prominent lumber barons who occupied it first.

English immigrant Charles Lee came to East Saginaw in 1862 after establishing a successful saw mill and brick works during the "building boom" in Detroit. He purchased two sawmills and 200 acres of pine lands in the Saginaw Valley for $40,000, an enormous sum of money at the time. He was also a director at the East Savings Bank and a major stockholder in the Saginaw-Tuscola and Huron Railroad. The red brick Queen Anne house was built by Lee in the 1870s. His house was the only lumber barons house built along the Saginaw River. The woodwork inside was supplied by his own sawmills. He was married three times (his first two wives died) and had eight children, seven of which were present when he died in the house in 1899. In 1911, Charles Duryea came to Saginaw. He built the first motor car in the United States in Springfield Massachusetts in 1892. Duryea used the old sawmill that was located behind the house to build his what he called a "motor buggy."

After Lee's death the house was purchased by Dr. Michael D. Ryan. He became the first resident physician at St. Mary's Hospital He would walk to lumber camps and sell the hospital's $5 insurance plans that would provide medical treatment for one year. Dr. Ryan was one of the last " horse and buggy" doctors traveling to outlying lumber camps in the Saginaw Valley. During the Great Fire of 1893 Dr. Ryan joined in the bucket brigade on the roof of St Mary's Hospital dousing embers from the fire saving the hospital from the treacherous flames. He was a staff physician for 55 years at St Mary's, and a charter member of the Michigan State Medical Society. He received a presidential citation for his work with the county draft board in WWI and WWII.

Dr. Ryan's daughter Rosemary married Roy DeGesero and they lived in the house raising their family in the same house she grew up in. When the Saginaw Daily News building was demolished in 1960 some of the terracotta lion heads that decorated the exterior were given to her, and prominently displayed on the front porch. Currently they are at the Castle Museum. Rosemary was an eccentric and interesting person, she loved the theater and often helped out at Pit and Balcony. She was known for her love of cats and had several of them. For those who did not know her name she was known as "the cat lady".

Sadly Rosemary died in 2012 a few years after moving to New Jersey to live with her daughter. The house went up for sale at that time and the City of Saginaw purchased the property and is the current owner.

Trip Tip: The Castle Museum is a few blocks to the north-east and displays the terracotta lion heads that once adorned the front porch of the "Cat Lady's House"

White Rock Lighthouse

Location: on the corner of White Rock Road and M-25

Before I get to the White Rock Memorial Light House, let's go way back to Michigan before the European explorers arrived in the Great Lake State. Off the Lake Huron shoreline, on the eastern part of the Thumb, stands an enormous white boulder. The rock was in the lake and protruded from the water. The native

Americans used it as a landmark. The town of White Rock, named after the landmark, grew as fur traders and trappers came to the area. By 1776, it was the largest village in the territory. It was used as a boundary marker for the northern point of the Treaty of Detroit with the Ottawa, Chippewa, Wyandot, and Potawatomi Native American nations which was signed on November 17 1807. In the 1830s, the town was a thriving port, and in 1856, a lighthouse was built to safely guide ships into port. The community, along with the lighthouse, was destroyed in the Great Fire of 1871. The devastating fire also occurred on the same day as the Great Chicago Fire, and while Chicago was rebuilt, White Rock never grew to be the large town it once was. Because it was no longer needed, the lighthouse was never rebuilt.

In 1996, a local resident of White Rock built a new house on M-23 that runs along the Lake Huron Shoreline. In honor of the original lighthouse they added a light tower to the new home. It's not an official aid to navigation sanctioned by the Coast Guard, but it still is nice to see a lighthouse looking over the great white rock that once guided the Michigan Native Americans so long ago.

The Lighthouse is a private residence, please be respectful to the owners.

Trip Tip: About a mile to the north of the lighthouse, there is a roadside park on the shore line of Lake Huron where you can see the "White Rock."

Michi Fact: After the Great Fire of 1871 in the Thumb the American Red Cross provided relief to the victims. This was the first relief effort by the newly- formed American Red Cross.

Mount Pleasant
Indian Industrial Boarding School

 **Location:** South Crawford Road near West Pickard Road. This is on tribal property where no trespassing is allowed and is strictly enforced, but you can get a good view of the buildings from South Crawford Road.

In the late 1800s, Alice Fletcher was the leader of a group of Americans that called themselves "Friends of the Indians". Their intent was not to socialize with the Native Americans but to convert them to Christianity and European American ways. In 1887 the Dawes Act, introduced by congressman Henry Dawes, created legislation that broke up the tribes and sectioned off their land giving each Indian land to farm. The United States government began to aggressively convert the Indians into American culture. One of the ways of doing that was removing the children from the tribes and reforming them at schools that were absent of Native American ideals.

The first building at the Mount Pleasant Indian Industrial Boarding School in Mt Pleasant was erected in 1892 for the purposes of educating Native American children. The eight classroom building opened to the first seventeen students in June of 1893. Enrollment had increased significantly and in the coming years it was necessary to build additional buildings to house all of the students and their daily activities. These included separate boys and girls dormitories, a hospital, a woodworking and blacksmith shop, a building for industrial training, a dining hall, a clubhouse for the employees of the school, and several farm buildings. During its operation the workers at the school physically abused many of the children and there are at least 174 undocumented children who died while attending the school.

The school closed on June 6, 1934, when the State of Michigan took over the property for Michigan Department of Mental Health services, and it became the Mount Pleasant branch of the Michigan Home and Training School. The intent of this home and training school was to house and train mentally handicapped young men. Many of the boys were abandoned, some were juvenile criminals that did not understand their crime or charges in court, some of the residence were physically handicapped, but a majority of the residents had some kind of mental health issue.

There are many rumors that it also housed the criminally insane including murderers and rapists. I think it gets confused with a correctional facility in Iowa called the Mount Pleasant Mental Health Institute, originally known as the Iowa Lunatic Asylum which opened in 1861.

Because if it's tragic history, many believe it to be haunted. It was designated as a State Historical Landmark in 1986 and you can see some of the buildings on Crawford Road. I took my photos from the road, since I was told it was patrolled and they watch closely for trespassers. Patrolled or not, I don't trespass and I would advise anyone against it.

Trip Tip: There is a historical marker for a Native American burial ground and cemetery on the west side of the property on Bamber Rd.

Santa House In Midland

Location: 359 West Main Sreet Midland, MI 48640

Ask any child and he/she will tell you Santa Claus lives at the North Pole, but he also has a house in downtown Midland. The house was constructed in the late 1980s and replaced a temporary structure that was set up for the holiday season and then taken down after the winter. The house is beautifully decorated with gingerbread molding, a glockenspiel and, of course, Christmas lights. This is a popular destination for children in mid-Michigan to visit with Santa and give him their list. For visitor information you can check out their website here http://www.midlandfoundation.org/santa-house

Michi-Fact: The house is used in October for the Charles W. Howard Santa Claus School. It's the only non-profit and oldest Santa School in the world.

Trip Tip: Dow Gardens and the Midland Center for the Arts is about a mile north of the Santa House, and the iconic Tridge over the Tittabawassee River and Chippewa River is a few blocks behind the Santa House.

Saginaw River Rear Range Lighthouse

Location: Located off Lighthouse Lane, North of Bay City on the west side of the Saginaw River, the lighthouse is on Dow Chemical property and is not open to the public. It can be seen by boat on the Saginaw River.

Sailing a ship into a river can be challenging if you don't know where the channel is that leads into the mouth of the river. To solve this problem, a pair of lights are placed in line with the channel. Captains can align the lights to sail straight into the river. Dewitt C. Brawn, 15-year-old son of the Saginaw River Lighthouse keeper, came up with the idea of having two lights for the captains to align. The Saginaw River was the first Lighthouse known as a "range" light. The system is now used throughout the world to guide ships into rivers.

The current lighthouse was built in 1876 in a swampy area north of Bay City and was deactivated in the 1960s, but was still used by the Coast Guard as living quarters until the 70s, when a new station was built across the river. Servicemen stationed at the decommissioned Lighthouse claimed to have heard strange sounds inside the old lighthouse, A Coast Guard Coastie reported hearing footsteps even though he was the only one there, and all the doors were locked.

The mystery of the footsteps are believed to be from one of two light keepers who died while serving at the lighthouse. Peter Brown was appointed Keeper of the old Lighthouse in 1866; being disabled he had help from his son and his wife Julia to maintain the light. He passed away in 1873 before the new range lights were built, but his family remained at the station, and Julia was placed in charge.

The new lighthouse was opened, and Julia served as head keeper until 1877, when George Way, whom Julia had married, was placed in charge of the light. Julia was made first assistant keeper, and served in this role until the position was deemed unnecessary by the government in October 1882. The position was reinstated the following spring, but the Coast Guard appointed Leonidus Charlton as first assistant keeper instead of Julia. Keeper Way died in November 1883, and sixty-seven-year old Julia left the station, which had been her home for seventeen years. There are rumors that Julia may have murdered her husbands, to be Head Lighthouse Keeper, but that has never been proven. Some believe it may be the spirits of the old lighthouse keepers who continue to haunt the old lighthouse remaining on duty for eternity.

Trip Tip: The lighthouse is open on special occasions such as the Tall Ship Celebration in Bay City. You can keep up on info about the lighthouse from the Saginaw River Marine Historical Society.

www.facebook.com/SaginawRiverMarineHistoricalSociety

Trip Tip. The U.S.S. Edson Navy Destroyer Museum ship is docked nearby on the Saginaw River and is available for tours.

Ladies of the Maccabees Building in Port Huron

Location: 901 Huron Avenue
Port Huron, MI 48060

North of downtown Port Huron is the massive Greek Revival building that is currently being used as a law office. I thought it was a former city hall or some other government building, but then I read "Ladies of the Maccabees" on the front. Now the question I had was *What is a Maccabee?*

The Knights of the Maccabees was a fraternal organization formed in London, Ontario. Started in 1878, it gained popularity in Michigan because it offered its members low-cost insurance. The Ladies of the Maccabees were the group's female auxiliary.

Bina Mae West was one of the Ladies of the Maccabees's most prominent members elevating the standard of living for women in the United States. At the age of eighteen she became a teacher and assistant principal at Capac High School. By the time she was 20, she won a seat on the Board of County School Examiners and was one of the first women in Michigan to hold an elected office. One day she attended a picnic sponsored by the Maccabees with her aunt. The fraternal benefit society was led by Port Huron native Nathan Boynton. The organization offered social and self-improvement activities as well as life and disability insurance at a time when neither was common. Benefit societies were a marvelous innovation with a fundamental flaw: They were for men only.

After two of her best pupils's mother had died without insurance, their father could not afford a nanny to take care of the children and had placed his daughter and son with a wealthy family to care for them. Instead of being taken in as members of the family the daughter served as a domestic servant and the son a stable boy. West felt women needed the opportunity to purchase life insurance and provide for their family after death. In 1892, she started the Woman's Benefit Association which is now the Woman's Life

Insurance Society. Over the next 56, years she built its membership from 319 in 1892 to 75,224 members in 42 states by 1900. Four years later, it had nearly 150,000 members and 40 employees at its Port Huron headquarters.

Bina Mae West was a supporter of women's right to vote and traveled the United States promoting woman's suffrage. In 1928, she was named the state's Top Businesswoman in a Detroit Free Press poll, and the Associated Press called her "one of the five greatest women in America."

I am glad that I saw that old building with the "Ladies of the Maccabees" chiseled into it. I never would have ever known about Bina Mae West and the remarkable life she lived.

Trip Tip: The Fort Gratiot Lighthouse is a few blocks to the east and the Huron Lightship is along the river walk.

Alonzo Hart Murder

Location: corner of North Woodbridge and East St. Charles Road northeast of Ithaca.

Among the farm fields of central Michigan is an old abandoned house between Ithaca and St. Charles. It has a tragic story to tell about the murder of it's owner Alonzo Hart Jr. in 1970. He was a Korean War Veteran and former Saginaw police officer who was working as a truck driver to support his family. His Second wife Sarah Jane Hart and her seventeen year-old lover, Phillip Lippert, hatched a plan to have him killed so she could collect the $18,000 insurance money. They found a killer for hire, William Pribble, that would commit the murder for $1,500. One night Alonzo's wife took the kids while Pribble and Lippert waited for Alonzo to return home, and when he pulled into the driveway, Pribble hit him over the head with a bar, and beat him to death, leaving him laying next to his car in the driveway.

Pribble and Lippert pled guilty to second degree murder, and each was given life sentences. Sarah Jane Hart, who was unable to remember details to help her attorney in her own defense ,was ultimately committed to a state mental hospital for 18 months before her first trial ended in a mistrial. The old, boarded up house still silently stands as a witness to this horrific crime.

Photo Tip: Old houses may look abandoned, but they are probably still owned by someone. I only photograph them from the road and advise against trespassing.

Hoyt Library

Location: 505 Janes Avenue, Saginaw, MI 48607

One of the key resources of knowledge in any community is the public library; and the castle-like Hoyt Library is no exception. Prominent businessman from New York Jesse Hoyt had lumbering interests in Saginaw. After his death in 1882, in his will he gave the city $100,000 dollars to construct a library. The architect firm of Van Brunt and Howe of Boston had their design selected, and the library was constructed with sandstone from Bay Port in the thumb, using a special railroad to transport the stone. The red limestone used to accent the building was supplied by quarries along Lake Superior. The interior was trimmed with oak paneling and beams along with an elegant stairway to the second floor. When it was opened in 1890 the grand structure was declared "the pride of all saginawians". The library is thought to be haunted, librarians have said that they have heard the sounds of old typewriters clicking away. They have also heard the sounds of books dropping from shelves late at night when no patrons are there, and when going to pick up the book there is none on the floor. One time a patron at the library told a librarian the old female librarian upstairs was really helpful although... there was no other librarian working up there at the time. A documentary of the hauntings titled *A Haunting at the Hoyt Library* was made by local film director Steven Shippy; you can find out more at their website www.hauntedsaginaw.com.

Trip Tip: The Castle Museum containing many artifacts from Michigan and Saginaw County, is next to the library and is open for tours for only one dollar.

MichiFact: Famed architect H.H. Richardson submitted a design for the library but it was rejected because it was said to have been too monumental and wasteful of space. The design was later used for the Howard Memorial Library in New Orleans. It was the last major architectural work before his death.

The Two Story Outhouse

Location: 7620 North Academy Road, Cedar Lake, MI It's on private property and not accessible to the public, but you can see it from the road.

Maybe you've heard the saying, "as dumb as a two-story outhouse." But hidden among the trees, in Cedar Lake, in central Michigan, is a tall historic two-story wooden outhouse. The house it sat behind was recently destroyed by fire. It's difficult to get a really good view of the old, weathered privy, but it is visible from the road. You can also see it from the nearby Fred Meijer Hartland Trail.

The two-story privy and house were built by William Nelson, a wealthy lumber baron who had seven daughters. The girls lived upstairs and the lower part of the home served as Mr Nelson's office and a general store that was frequented by lumberjacks. The lumber baron wanted to keep his daughters separated from the men so he built the outhouse with a bridge (which collapsed in the 50s) to the second floor of the home.

The outhouse has four different size holes to match four different size derrieres. The holes on the top are off-set from the holes on the bottom. A wooden panel behind the bottom set of holes separates the waste from the occupants at the bottom, giving a whole new meaning to the term "poop chute"

Trip Tip: The Fred Meijer Heartland Trail passes next to the property the old Outhouse is standing on. There are parking lots for the trail at Edmore, Vestaburg and Riverdale.

The Big Brick Flag of Little Michigan

Location: on the west side of I-75 a few miles north of the I-75 and US-10 interchange

The people on the west side of the state probably won't recognize this brick flag, but the people on the east side of the state who travel I-75 will recognize it standing along the highway near Bay City. It has the 50-state design on one side, and the bicentennial design with the circle of stars on the other. For some, it marks the dividing line of "Up North" on the traveling to northern Michigan, and for others, it means they are almost home when heading south. The flag was built in 1975 by local bay city businessman, Jim Graham, as a way to promote an amusement park he wanted to build called "Little Michigan". The park was supposed to be in the shape of Michigan with ponds in the shape of the five Great Lakes. The park never did get built, but the flag still stands, waving at motorists as they drive by.

MichiFact: I-75 is the seventh longest Interstate Highway, the second longest north-south after I-95, and passes through six different states: Florida, Georgia, Tennessee, Kentucky, Ohio, and, of course, Michigan. The northern end of I-75 is at Sault St. Marie

The Ghost Town of Melbourne

An old pump shack in the area where the town of Melbourne used to be

Location: The exact location of the town is not known, but it was next to the Saginaw River on Melbourne Road North of Zillwaukee.

The town of Melbourne was founded by Wellington R. Burt in 1867 along the Saginaw River with a station located on the Saginaw and Mackinac Railroad line that ran between Saginaw and Bay City. Burt had recently visited Australia and liked the city of Melbourne, so he named the town after the city. According to some old maps I found, the town, which no longer remains, was on Melbourne road a few miles north of an existing concrete plant. The Sawmill in Melbourne was said to be the largest sawmill in the world at the time. I am not sure if that is true, but there were several saw mills in the town besides Burt's, along with a shingle mill, a barrel works, and a salt processing plant. There were about 50 houses and some barracks for the unmarried workers, and a library and a school for the workers children. In 1877, the town suffered from a devastating fire, but it did not completely wiped the town off the face of the earth, like some reports I have found stated, I think at that point, Wellington Burt did not want to rebuild his sawmill. After the fire, David Whitney Jr. of Detroit and Henry Batchelor of Bay City built a sawmill in Melbourne, along with a salt works and barrel plant. The sawmill produced over 30,000,000 feet of lumber a year.

A famous resident of Melbourne was George "Kid" Lavigne who's parents moved from Bay City to Melbourne in 1880 where his father worked at Whitney and Batchelor, and in his youth, George worked as a cooper making barrels to ship salt. Lavigne, also known as "The Saginaw Kid," was boxing's first widely recognized World Lightweight champion when he won the title in 1896.

Melbourne was destroyed by another fire in 1894, and they made the decision not to rebuild the mill. By then the lumber industry was slowing down with much of the white pine trees in the Saginaw Valley gone.

After the devastating fire of 1894, the company sold the remaining houses for a few dollars to anyone who wanted to move them a few miles to Zilwaukee. In the early 1900s, an amusement park named Melbourne Park was built but it went out of business a few years later. Strangely, it was used as a nudist colony for a short time, but apparently the cold Michigan weather was not a suitable climate for such a thing. Nothing remains of the town of Melbourne today; but, who knows, maybe someone in Zilwaukee is living in George "Kid" Lavigne's old house.

Michi-Fact: George "The Saginaw Kid" Lavigne was inducted into the International Boxing Hall of Fame in 1998.

Lost In Michigan

Chapter 3
Northern Lower Peninsula

The Historic Manistee Fire Station

Location: 281 First Street
Manistee, MI 49660

After the devastating fire of 1871 that swept across Michigan, most of Manistee was destroyed, and a new fire station was quickly built but was not sufficient to meet the needs of the town. The current fire station that stands today replaced the inadequate one built after the fire.

In early October 1888, the Manistee City Council hired Frederick Hollister of Saginaw, the architect who also designed Manistee's school, to design a grand fire hall to replace the original station to serve the community for generations. The formidable building was constructed of brick, cut-stone, and French plate glass trimmed with galvanized iron. This Romanesque Revival-style building was constructed by the local firm of Brownrigg and Reynolds at a cost of $7,516. A copper covered dome tops the tower that rises above the city of Manistee on this architectural treasure. The new station opened in June 1889 when a horse-drawn steam engine was brought from the original hall. The fire fighting equipment has changed over the years, but the ever vigilant fire station is the oldest continually operating fire station in Michigan.

Michifact: Manistee is an Ojibwa term meaning "Spirit of the Woods"

Trip Tip: The Manistee North Pierhead Light, at the mouth of the Manistee River, is not far away from the hall

Grousehaven Lodge in the Rifle River Recreation Area

Location: 2550 Rose City Road, Lupton, MI 48635

Inside the Rifle River Recreation Area next to the Jewett Observation tower are the remains from the old Grousehaven Lodge. All that is left from the lodge is an old basement or wine cellar. It's a little tricky to find unless you know where to look. There is a guardrail in the parking area south of the observation tower, and the cellar is underneath the parking area. If you hike around the guardrail and go down the hill you will see the doorway to the left.

Harry Mulford "Hal" Jewett was born in Elmira, NY in 1870 and was a world class athlete for the University of Notre Dame. He was a two-time U.S. national champion, and he set the American record for the 220 yard dash in 1891, and in the triple jump in 1890. He also equaled the World Record for the 220-yard dash in 1892. He scored the very first touchdown for Notre Dame Football in a game against the University of Michigan on April 20, 1888. Michigan won the Game 26-6. It is said that the Wolverine fans in Ann Arbor were upset that the team was scored on by Notre Dame since it was the first time in over four years Michigan had allowed an opposing team to get a touchdown.

After graduating from college and serving in the Navy during the Spanish-American War he eventually became the president of Paige Motor Car Company in Detroit. Paige even built a low-price model named after the president of the company called the *Jewett.*

In the 1920s, Jewett was looking for a place to take his dogs and their trainers to hunt. He fell in love with the area near Lupton and purchased 7,000 acres of land. He eventually built an enormous lodge, bringing in Finnish "axemen" from the Upper Peninsula to fell and trim the logs for the construction of the lodge. Workers were brought in from the Detroit area, and overcoming the difficulties of limited resources in the rural area, the large two-story log lodge was built with all the modern conveniences, including steam heat, electric lights, a private bath and a large living room featuring a huge fireplace. There was also an observation room on the roof with a spectacular view of the area.

Hunting ruffed grouse, partridge, and pheasant made the area a world-class preserve. He also worked with the U.S. Bureau of Fisheries in stocking the headwaters of the Rifle River with trout, making it one of the best fishing areas in the state. It was reported that Jewett had spent over a quarter of a million dollars on Grousehaven's Lodge and its preserve.

When Harry Jewett suddenly died of a heart attack in 1933, his heirs lost interest in Grousehaven, and in 1945, it was sold to the state of Michigan for $75,000. It was used by the Department of Conservation for fish and game research. In 1963 the lands were deeded over to the Parks Division and the lodge was torn down in 1967. You can still find some of the remains of the lodge, which I think used to be the fireplace, near the observation tower that stands between Lodge Lake and Grebe Lake.

MichiFact: The notorious Purple Gang from Detroit frequented the area, and it's believed by some that they used Grousehaven to conduct business and get away from authorities.

Five Channels Dam

Location: on M-65 where it crosses the Au Sable River

I like to stop and get a dam photo (no pun intended) whenever I am near one of Michigan's 2,500 dams. If I am lucky the spill way is open and it's like getting a photo of a waterfall. One of the largest dams in Michigan is the Five Channels Dam near Oscoda on the Au Sable River. In 1911, the newly-formed Consumers Power Company, formed by the Foote brothers from Jackson Michigan, built the Five Channels Dam; it was the second of six hydroelectric dams to be built on the

Au Sable River. The dam is located, where, at one time, five channels flowed into the river giving the dam its name.

During the construction of the Panama Canal, and the challenge conditions for the workers, the health and safety of the workers became a priority. When building the dam the company wanted to provide a good working environment for their workers and built a forty-five acre camp with a central water system, a school, a washroom, and a store. Workers also were given land to build a house on. After the dam was complete the "work town" was moved to Loud Dam site, the next dam to be built on the Au Sable River. Because of its ground-breaking approach to worker health and safety, the site was placed on the national register of historic places in March of 2002.

Michifact: The first hydroelectric power plant in the country was in Grand Rapids at the Wolverine Chair Factory. A water turbine was used to power sixteen carbon arc street lamps on July 24, 1880.

Trip Tip: Iargo Springs and Lumberman's Monument in the Huron National Forest are only a few miles away on River Road.

Tawas Point Lighthouse

Location: inside the Tawas Point State Park 686 Tawas Beach Road, East Tawas, MI 48730

In the early 1800s Tawas Point was a potential hazard to ships entering Tawas bay at night or during a storm. The point was originally known as Ottawa Point named after Chief O-ta-was of the Saginaw Chippewa tribe, but eventually the point was changed to Tawas to sound more like the chief's name. In 1850 congress approved a lighthouse to be built at the point to guide ships, and a 45-foot-tall stone tower was constructed along with a small keepers' dwelling. By 1869, the old lighthouse began to fall apart, with the roof leaking and the floors needing replacement. Sailors complained that the light from the tower was dimly lit and was not visible during a storm. Because the point continually changes with the blowing sands, the light was no longer at the tip of the point, so the decision was made to construct a new lighthouse in 1876 and is the same one still standing today.

The new tower is 67 feet tall and has a 4th Order Fresnel Lens that can be seen for 16 miles. By 1953, the lighthouse was automated and was no longer staffed. In 1996, the Coast Guard sold the lighthouse to the Michigan Department of Natural Resources, although the Coast Guard still owns the actual lantern as it is an aid to navigation. It is one of the few lighthouses in the nation still using the old original lens but the Coast Guard has said they wish to replace it with a modern lantern.

Lighthouse tours are available for $5 per person from May to October and you can also volunteer to be a lighthouse keeper living at the lighthouse and giving tours to visitors. for more information check out:
www.michigan.gov/tawaslighthouse

MichiFact: The lighthouse at Milliken State Park and Harbor in Detroit is a replica of the Tawas Point Tower.

Our Lady of the Woods Shrine in Mio

Location: 100 Deyarmond Street, Mio, MI 48647

The town of Mio is where M-72 crosses M-33 in the northern lower peninsula and near that intersection is a majestic stone mountain with Christian statues and gorgeous landscaping full of plants and flowers.

The Our Lady of the Woods Shrine at St Mary's Catholic Church in Mio was constructed by Rev. Hubert Rakowski between 1953 and 1955 with the support of the local community. The grounds are open year round and the landscaping in the summer is breathtaking. Photos can not capture the size and beauty of this impressive shrine. If you are ever in the area I highly recommend stopping to see it.

MichiFact: Mio was named Mioe after Mioe Deyarmond, one of its founder's wives. The town was given a post office in 1882. I am not sure why but the "e" was dropped and the town was changed to Mio in 1883.

Mio holds the record for the highest recorded temperature in Michigan at 112 degrees Fahrenheit on July 13, 1936.

Trip Tip: The Mio Hydroelectric Plant and historical marker are a few miles north of Mio where M-33 crosses the Au Sable River.

Woolsey Memorial Airport

 **Location:** 13591 East Woolsey Lake Road, Northport, MI 49670

Near the tip of the Leelanau Peninsula, north of Northport, the main road passes by the Clinton F. Woolsey Memorial Airport. It's hard to miss the fascinating stone building with a black and yellow "bumble bee" yellow and black striped roof.

Clinton F. Woolsey was born in 1894 in Northport and grew up on his family farm. He took a great interest in anything mechanical, and after finishing school in Northport, he studied engineering at Valparaiso University in Indiana. After college, he enlisted in the military eventually becoming a test pilot. While in the military, he trained pilots and one of his students was Charles Lindbergh, the first person to fly solo across the Atlantic Ocean. Clinton was working on a plane he nicknamed the "Woolsey Bomber" and planned to be the first to fly non stop over the Atlantic ocean, but he was called into duty for the Pan-American Goodwill Flight to promote American aviation in Central and South America in 1926 and 1927.

He oversaw the construction and testing of the five Loening OA-1 amphibian observation planes to be used on the tour. Tragically he was killed on the tour when his plane collided with another plane in the clouds on February 26 1927 in Buenos Aires. After the collision, co-plot John W. Benton climbed out onto the wing without a parachute to try to lower the damaged landing gear. Captain Woolsey could have probably parachuted to safety but chose to pilot the plane with Benton on the wing. Without being able to lower the landing gear, the plane crashed and both men were killed. "I have never witnessed a more courageous sacrifice," said Capt. Ira Eaker, who witnessed the crash from his plane.

In 1934, during the Great Depression, Capt. Woolsey's 85-year-old father Byron Woolsey wanted to ensure that Clinton would always be remembered. He donated 80 acres of his land to Leelanau Township on the condition it be used as an airport in honor of his son. The township added another 120 acres. A Works Progress Administration crew converted the farm, as part of a "New Deal" Public Works Project, into a long grassy runway and expanded Woolsey's creamery/milk transfer station into a terminal. The Northport Woman's Club donated a bronze plaque honoring Capt. Woolsey, which was placed on a large boulder near the terminal.

Trip Tip: The airport is not far from the Grand Traverse Lighthouse at the tip of the Leelenau Peninsula in the Leelenau State Park.

Rolling Up Hill Near Rose City

Location: Reasner Road north of Heath Road

Northeast of Rose City, on Reasner Road, at the bottom of the hill if you stop and put your car in neutral, it will roll up hill.

While I was near Rose City, I had to check out the "gravity hill" on Reasner Road. I was not sure what part of the road the hill was on until I came near the end of the road and saw a sign that read "Do Not Stop, Do Not Go Backwards." they put up a sign telling someone not to do it, and I could not resist the temptation of going to jail just to try out the gravity hill. I figure the deer on the side of the road would not mind either, so I put the Jeep in neutral, and it sure felt like I was going up hill. Now I know gravity does not work backwards, and it's more of an optical illusion, but it sure seemed like I broke Issac Newtons Laws.

I don't recommend you to do it, because you are probably breaking some sort of motor vehicle law, but I thought I would share my experience with you.

Trip Tip: About five miles to the east of Rose City is the Rifle River Recreation Area. It's located within the AuSable State Forest and provides a variety of recreational opportunities such as wildlife watching, hiking, fishing, and camping.

Alden Train Depot

Location: 10670 Coy St, Alden, MI 49612

Nestled on the southeastern shore of Torch Lake Alden is a quaint little midwestern town and a great place to visit for that nastalgic feeling of times gone by. The tracks are gone now but at one time the railroad passed through the town of Alden and the Pere Marquette Railway built a charming little depot in 1907 to replace the one that burned in 1906. Northern Michigan newspapers called it "the railroad's finest depot north of Grand Rapids". William Alden Smith, the railway's general counsel, proposed the rail line between Traverse City and Petoskey. In 1891, the town was renamed Alden in his honor. It was originally called Spencer Creek named after the creek in the area that flows into Torch Lake. In 1981, the last train left Alden and the railroad let the old station sit empty and abandoned. Helena Township acquired the depot in 1986 and restored it to it's present glory.

Many tourists over the years have come to Alden and disembarked the train at the station. Although the train no longer travels through Alden it is still a wonderful tourist destination with shops, restaurants, and the Alden Mill House selling Chef Geno's special blends of Spices and seasonings. If you're in the Traverse City area the town of Alden is the perfect place to visit for a day trip.

Trip Tip: The route through Alden, Bellaire and Boyne City makes an excellent trip between Traverse City and Petoskey that meanders through some beautiful countryside of Michigan.

Photo Tip: Taking less-traveled back roads makes it easier to stop and take a photograph if you find something interesting. Just be careful stopping on hills or corners so that cars can see you on the side of the road.

The Old Petoskey Library

Location: 451 East Mitchell Street. Petoskey, MI 49770

Among all the wonderful shops and restaurants in downtown Petoskey is the old public library. Andrew Carnegie promised $12,500 if the citizens of Petoskey would provide the land for the library and the funds to maintain it. Mrs. Lelia Johnson purchased the present site in memory of her husband, and presented it to the city under the condition that the site would always be used as a library. After raising an additional $5,000, this magnificent library building was constructed in 1908.

There were several Carnegie Libraries built around the country, but this one has the distinction of being a favorite of a literary icon, young Ernest Hemingway, who would spend his summers at his family's vacation cottage on nearby Walloon Lake.

Near the sidewalk, in front of the grand old library, is a sign that reads:

When living in Petoskey in 1919 the library was a favorite haunt of Hemingway's and, in December, wearing his Italian cape and Red Cross uniform, he spoke here to the Ladies Aid Society about his World War I experiences. At that event he met the Connable family who led to his connection with the Toronto Star newspaper and his employment as its European Correspondent.

Trip Tip: Make sure you have change for the parking meters downtown. If you don't mind doing a little walking, on busy days it's easier to park at Bay Front Park and take the walk way to downtown.

Ocqueoc Falls

Location: M-68 nine miles west of Rogers City

While most Michiganders are familiar with some of the waterfalls in the Upper Peninsula many do not realize there are a few of these natural wonders in the Lower Peninsula as well. Not far from Rogers City on the east side of the mitten is the largest waterfall in the Lower Peninsula is Ocqueoc falls (pronounced Ah-key-ock) on the Ocqueoc River between Onaway and Rogers City. The word

Ocqueoc comes from a French term meaning "crooked waters" and is one of the few rivers in Lower Michigan to flow north. There is a nice parking lot off M-68 and the falls are easily accessible with a short walk. Besides the waterfalls, you can hike or bike the Ocqueoc Falls Bicentennial Pathway with its miles of trails that wind through the woods along the river.

Wreck Of The Joseph S. Fay

Location: 7323 US Highway 23 N, Rogers City, 49779 The wreck lies on the shoreline in front of the 40 Mile Point Lighthouse

The average person does not get to see a Great Lakes shipwreck since most lie at the bottom of the lakes. On the shoreline of Lake Huron there is a chance to look at the remains of a wooden steamship that sailed the great lakes.

The lighthouse keeper's log at 40 Mile Point for October 20, 1905 simply reads: "At 8:30 p.m. last night the steamer, *J.S. Fay*, came ashore here in a sinking condition. She soon broke up. Most of the crew came ashore on the Pilot House. Three men swam ashore, the mate was drowned." The entry for December 4, 1905 reads: "The assistant found a dead man on the beach about 1 mile up. We think it is the mate of the Fay."

The *Joseph S. Fay* was a wooden steamer built in 1871 and was one of the first Great Lakes freighters built for the iron ore trade. On October 19, 1905, in heavy seas, the *Fay* with the *Rhodes* in tow, departed from Escanaba, Michigan and was downbound on Lake Huron. The captain hugged the coast seeking some protection from the violent wind and savage waves. The wind shifted violently straining the towline tightened, pulling it taut until the *Rhodes* broke free taking a portion of the *Fay's* stern with her.

Water rushed into the hull and the crew crowded into the forward cabin. The captain struggled to bring the Fay around and head to shore toward 40 Mile Point Light Station. Her bow struck a sandbar and the entire forward cabin was torn off. The wheelhouse and captain's room were ripped from the deck. Incredibly, huge waves lifted

106

the structure and carried it to shore where it washed up on the sandy beach near the light station. The captain and 10 crewmen were safe inside. In fact, one of the crewmen was reported to be asleep and didn't even wake up.

First Mate David Syze of Port Huron and two other crewmen weren't so fortunate. Clinging to the beached hull, the struggling men ripped off a spar and used it to paddle to shore. The first mate attempted to swim, but was overcome by the cold and was lost.

Trip Tip: The 40 Mile Point Lighthouse is open with free admission from Memorial Day weekend through mid-October and besides the Lighthouse and the wreck of the *Joseph S. Fay,* they have the pilot house from the *Calcite* freighter on display too.

Seven Bridges Recreation Area

Location: Valley Road Between Kalkaska and Rapid City

For years the people living around Kalkaska would visit the idyllic little park off Valley Road and enjoy meandering the trails and foot bridges that crossed the winding Rapid River. There was a simple wooden sign that welcomed visitors and asked them not to litter, build camp fires or pick the wild flowers. What visitors did not know was that the park was privately owned and that the owner was kind enough to open the property up for people to enjoy.

Gordon Peschke and his siblings had inherited the property that his great uncles had build a sawmill on in 1882 after their parents had purchased the land of which the deed was signed by Ulysses S Grant. Mr Peschke loved the property and built little bridges across the river and planted trees to replace the ones the lumberjacks cut down. Over the years the trees grew and Michiganders would come to picnic underneath the cedar trees or fish in the clear waters of the river. As Gordon and his siblings grew older they were no longer able to care for the property and the taxes became a burden.

In the early 1980's Gordon worked out a deal with the AuSable Institute in Grayling to purchase the land for $90,000, about half of what it was valued at, to use it for educational purposes but the institute was not able to raise the money.

Gordon wanted to give the property away but his siblings made the decision to sell to some real estate developers for $180,000 to divide the property up into a housing development.

While visiting the property with a friend Helen Milliken, wife of former governor Milliken, she noticed the survey markers and inquired about why they were there. After finding out about the housing plans Mrs. Milliken worked with Grand Traverse Regional Land Conservancy and Lansing to purchase the property and in 1995 it officially became public property and the Seven Bridges Recreation Area.

It's not a large area compared to some of the state parks, the Seven Bridges area is about 300 acres and the foot bridges and little waterfalls are not far from the parking lot. It is easily accessible for anyone to enjoy.

PhotoTip: Cloudy days are good days to take photographs in the woods so you don't get bright spots and dark shadow spots under the trees.

Middle Village

Location: 23 North Lamkin Road, Harbor Springs, MI 49740

Half way between Harbor springs and Cross Village on M-119 is Middle Village. It can be a little tricky to find but if you turn onto Lamkin Road near the Good Hart General Store it will take you back to the village where you will see the beautiful little country church of St Ignatius.

Rows of simple wooden crosses marks the Odawa Indians laid to rest in the Middle Village Cemetery. The village started in 1741 as a settlement of Jesuit Missionaries and Native Americans, who called the area "Apatawaaing," or Middle Village.

Next to the church is a trail that leads to Middle Village Park Beach on Lake Michigan. The park also has an overlook that is open all year long.

The village is along the " Tunnel of Trees" route that follows the shore line of lake Michigan and is a popular route for tourists, especially during the autumn season.

Trip Tip: Lamkin Road south of Middle Village becomes narrow and steep, it's recommended that you come in from Good Hart and head back out that direction.

Cheboygan Lighthouse Ruins

Location: 4490 Beach Road, Cheboygan, MI 49721 inside the Cheboygan State Park

Along the shores of Lake Huron in the Cheboygan State park is the ruins of the old Cheboygan Point Lighthouse. The first light at Cheboygan Point was built in 1851. There was a dwelling and a separate 40' round brick tower, which was fitted with a Fifth Order Fresnel lens made by L. Saultier & Company of Paris. The light was built on a pier and after only eight years of service, high water was washing away at the foundation and the light tower was removed.

In 1859 the station was rebuilt as an eight foot square wooden tower resting atop a two story eight room dwelling. The new tower rose 22 feet above the house and included the same white light which was used in the earlier tower. In May of 1890, a standard locomotive steam fog signal was installed in a separate building.

When the nearby Fourteen Foot Shoal Light was constructed offshore in 1930, the old Cheboygan Light Station was abandoned and the land was deeded to the State of Michigan. Following vandalism, the buildings were dismantled in the 1940s when George Kling, son of Fred Kling, the last keeper of the lighthouse, purchased the station's boathouse for $1 and moved it to his home in Cheboygan to serve as a garage. Bill Singer acquired the lighthouse and sold its materials to Bert Toles, who used them to build three small houses. All that remains today is the foundation from the old lighthouse, which you can see along the hiking trails at Cheboygan state park.

Besides guiding ships through the straits of Mackinaw the lighthouse marked the entrance to Duncan Bay and Duncan City on the opposite side of the bay from the lighthouse. Once the county seat of Cheboygan County (1853-1857), named after Jeremiah Duncan who started lumbering in the area the city was a company town with a population of about 500 in its heyday, and also a refuelling stop for Great Lakes steamships. Duncan City began to lose its importance when the Cheboygan River was dredged out deeper, thus allowing more shipping traffic to go to Cheboygan itself. The final blow for Duncan City came in 1898 when the sawmill burned to the ground. The property is now all residential and privately owned and nothing remains of the city today.

Trip Tip: Fourteen Foot Shoals Lighthouse and Poe Reef Lighthouse are visible from the shoreline at the old lighthouse in the state park.

Photo Tip: if you have a camera with a long telephoto lens you can zoom out and get some decent photos of Poe Reef Lighthouse off shore in Lake Huron.

McGulpin Point Lighthouse

Location: 500 Headlands Road
Mackinaw City, MI 49701

A few miles west of Mackinaw City is the McGulpin Point Lighthouse that was built in 1869. The lighthouse is the same design that was used at Eagle Harbor and White River. For 27 years, James Davenport was the light keeper that maintained the lighthouse and sent in ice reports to the district inspector in Milwaukee.

During the end of the Great Lakes shipping season in December of 1893 Keeper Davenport took a trip to Mackinaw City, Since his wife had died a few years earlier he left his nine children in charge of the lighthouse. While he was gone the wooden propeller driven steamer *Waldo*

A. Avery burst into flames in the Straights of Mackinaw. In a desperate attempt to save the crew the captain beached the ship at McGulpin point near the lighthouse. The lifeboats were destroyed by the fire and the crew could not use them to get to shore in the icy waters of Lake Michigan. The keepers resourceful children used the lighthouse skiff to rescue all 17 sailors aboard what was left of the *Waldo A. Avery*. The remains of the ship was recovered and towed to Bay City where it was rebuilt and named the *Phenix*.

By 1906, the lighthouse board decided the light was not necessary because of the Mackinaw Point Lighthouse in Mackinaw City. The lighthouse was *decommissioned* and the lantern was removed. The house was sold to a private owner and remained in private ownership for many years. After the most recent owner passed away the lighthouse was purchased in 2008 by Emmet County and is open to the public for tours. Visitors can climb the tower to get a spectacular view of the Mackinaw Bridge. When you are in Mackinaw City you need to visit the old lighthouse. Take W. Central Ave, the main road through town, west and you will see a sign for the lighthouse.

Trip Tip: A few miles to the south down Wilderness Park Drive there is a public beach that faces west on Lake Michigan for a wonderful view of the sunset. After the sunset you can visit the nearby Dark Sky Park to see the stars. You will need a red-colored light as white lights are banned from the park to allow for viewing of the night sky.

Lost In Michigan

Chapter 4
Upper Peninsula

Fort Mackinac Post Cemetery

Location: Garrison Road Mackinac Island 49757

Mackinac Island is one of the most popular tourist destinations in Michigan for it breathtaking beauty, quaint shops, and delicious fudge. There is also a lot of American history to experience on the island and one of the lesser visited places is Post Cemetery near the center of the island. It is one of only four National Cemeteries with the honor of permanently flying the American flag at half mast and is the final resting place for Fort Mackinac soldiers, their families, and local officials. The small piece of land on Mackinac Island is surrounded by a white picket fence with a wooden archway, and has a canon from Fort Sumter, South Carolina on display. Of the approximately 108 burials in Fort Mackinac Post Cemetery, 69 are unknown. The origin of the property is lost to poor record keeping in the early 1800's but local lore from the nineteenth century suggests that both American and British War of 1812 soldiers are buried here. Many early burials were marked with simple wooden crosses that have long since decayed and disappeared. As a result many of the burials are unknown.

Among the buried is German-born Civil war veteran Ignatius Goldhofer who came to Fort Mackinac in 1896 with a variety of ailments and old wounds. When he died three years later, his wife and four children buried him in the Post Cemetery.

Civilian interments include Edward Biddle who served the community as sheriff, village president and surveyor in the mid nineteenth century. In the 1880s Lieutenant Calvin Cowles and his wife Mary buried their infant children Josiah and Isabel next to each other in the shaded northeast corner.

In case you are wondering, the other cemeteries that are authorized to fly the flag permanently at half mast are the National Memorial Cemetery of the Pacific (the Punchbowl) in Honolulu, Hawaii; Arlington National

Cemetery in Arlington, Virginia; and National Cemetery at Gettysburg in Gettysburg, Pennsylvania.

Trip Tip:: The carriage tours will ride past the cemetery, or you can walk up Fort Street to Custer Road to Fort Service Road. It's not a far walk, but it is a steep one. From the cemetery you can walk past Skull Cave and Fort Holmes and to Arch Rock.

The Haunted Ghost Town of Shelldrake

Location: about 2 miles north of Paradise on private property not accessible to the public

The town of Shelldrake, named after a duck common in the area, is a ghost town at the mouth of the Shelldrake River (also known as the Betsy River) on Whitefish Bay. In the 1890s and early 1900s, it was a thriving sawmill town during the peak logging years on the Tahquamenon River.

By the 1920s, repeated fires and the decline of lumbering led to its demise. Today, it is a privately-owned ghost town with only a few weathered, original buildings.

There are stories of the area being haunted by an old sea captain who stands on the dock. He has a pipe and a cape, and he is usually seen from the lake. As boats approach the shore, he fades away and disappears. The tugboat Grace, which was towing a barge in October of 1879 through Whitefish Bay was headed for Goulais Bay in Canada. During a storm in the early morning, the tugboat broke down and drifted onto a sand bar about 200 feet offshore from Shelldrake. The tug filled with water and broke to pieces. The crew made it to shore, and after climbing the bank to safety the captain proclaimed, "Thank God, we are all safe." and then suddenly dropped dead of a heart attack. This may be the captain's ghost that has been seen on the docks.

By the late 1890s, Shelldrake had a sawmill, houses for workers that were equipped with bathrooms, a hospital, a school house, a post office, and an icehouse that could store enough meat to feed a population of 1,000 through the winter months. All of the buildings were plastered and had hot water piped from the sawdust burner. There was a stagecoach that ran between Shelldrake and Eckerman, about twenty miles to the south, daily in the summer and three times a week during the winter. At one time there was also a passenger ship sailing between Shelldrake and Sault Ste. Marie, Michigan.

The Penoyer brothers from Bay City, Michigan began the first lumbering operations on the mouth of the Shelldrake River in 1895 with the construction of a sawmill, long docks, and a tramway into Whitefish Bay for loading lumber onto ships. They owned a large block of pine lands in the Tahquamenon River watershed. The Calumet and Hecla Mining Company bought the sawmill and uncut timber in 1899 for construction of their mines. Calumet and Hecla sold out to a Canadian firm, the Bartlett Brothers, in 1910. Lumber milling continued at Shelldrake until 1925 when a fire burned down the sawmill plant for the second time.

Shelldrake was listed on Michigan's Historic Register in 1979 with the period of historical significance designated as 1600–1825. However, Shelldrake did not become settled as a lumber town until the late 1890s. The state marker text reads:

Shelldrake legend has it that Lewis Cass, governor of the Territory of Michigan, and his party of nearly 100 camped here in their search for the source of the Mississippi River in 1820. This area, once a bustling lumbering community, was first settled in the mid-nineteenth century. Shelldrake is now a sleepy resort and hunting place. Few of the weather beaten buildings that once faced the long boardwalk remain. This settlement is a reminder of

*the area's lumbering era. Although Shelldrake was
sold to private owners during the 1930s, it never
developed into a resort or hunting place despite
what is recorded on the Michigan historic marker.
It is now a privately owned ghost town with only a
few weathered, original buildings at the site.*

Trip Tip: Unfortunately you can't visit the town of
Shelldrake, but Whitefish Point Lighthouse is nearby and
Tahquamenon upper and lower falls are a few miles west of
Paradise on M-123

The King of the File Folder's
Mackinac Island Cottage

Location: 8009 West Bluff Road
Mackinac Island

Coming into Mackinac Island on the
ferry there is an excellent view of the
Grand Hotel that looks out over Lake Huron. To the west
of the iconic hotel is a row of stately old summer homes on
what is known as the West Bluff. One of those cottages
was owned by the man who invented the file folder.

The first house built on this lot in 1886 was constructed by
William Westover Jr., a lumber baron from Bay City,
Michigan. He sold the cottage to Chicago businessman
William Amberg, who was the inventor of a file folder
system and with his great fortune, he and his wife, Sarah
Agnes Ward, purchased the West Bluff's Westover cottage
on Mackinac Island. They demolished the cottage in 1892
and built the one still standing today calling it, Inselheim
which is German for "Island Home", but eventually
renamed it to Edgecliff Cottage. Some referred to it as the
Wedding Cake Cottage because of the decorative
woodwork that resembles cake icing.

Mr. Amberg was known as "King of the File Folders" as
owner of the Amberg File & Index Co. In 1868, he devised
a system of flat folders and filing drawers to store the
folders, acquiring 30 patents and over 600 copyrights.

Before his invention, papers and documents would be rolled and tied up with a ribbon and placed in slot that became known as "pigeon holes." Amberg's company prospered until 1897 when another company started making a similar folder, and after an argument was made in court where the judge ruled that William Amberg did not own the sole rights to the file folder system. Although the king was dethroned, he must have still made out pretty well on his folders to have such a beautiful place on Mackinac Island.

Trip Tip: To get to the west bluff of Mackinac Island, you have to walk around behind the Grand Hotel on Algonquin Street. The staff at the hotel will not let you pass in front of the hotel unless you are a guest.

MichiFact: Michigan governor G. Mennen "Soapy" Williams built a mansion on the west bluff, now known as the Foundation House. He is laid to rest in Protestant Cemetery on Mackinac Island.

Luce County Sheriff's House and Jail

Location: 411 West Harrie Street in Newberry 49868

Compared to cities in the lower peninsula like Detroit, Grand Rapids, or Lansing, Newberry is not that large of a city, but for the Upper Peninsula, Newberry is one of the larger towns. In the middle of the eastern half of the U.P. it's kind of a hub for many tourist destinations, with the Tahquamenon Falls and Whitefish Point to the north-east, and Pictured Rocks National Lakeshore to the north-west. If you're in Newberry, a little bit off the main road, about 4 blocks west of M-123 on Harrie street is the old Newberry Jail and Sheriff's residence. Constructed in 1894, the massive brick Queen Anne style house served as the Luce County jail and sheriff's residence for over seventy years. The Peninsular Land Company donated the land for the site, and the architectural firm of Lovejoy and DeMar from Marquette designed this beautiful building, built with rough-hewn Jacobsville sandstone. Luce County Historical Society rescued this building from demolition in 1975 and restored it as the Luce County Historical Museum in 1976. If you want to visit the museum you can find out the hours it is open on the Luce County Historical Society Facebook page here: https://www.facebook.com/lucecountyhistoricalsociety/

The village of Newberry was founded in 1882 as the logging headquarters for the Vulcan Furnace Company. Originally it was called Grant's Corners, but it was renamed in honor of John Stoughton Newberry, a U.S. Representative and industrialist from Detroit, who was instrumental in bringing the railroad through the Upper Peninsula town.

MichiFact:: Newberry was designated as the moose capital of Michigan by the state legislature, in House Resolution 2002-572 and Senate Resolution 2002-259.

Big Bay Point Lighthouse

Location: #3 Lighthouse Road, Big Bay, Michigan 49808

Standing on a tall, rocky bluff overlooking Lake Superior is the Big Bay Point Lighthouse, built in 1897 near the town of Big Bay. The house was built as a duplex with one side for the head lighthouse keeper and the other for the assistant keeper. Those who worked at Big Bay Point were truly isolated, and the keepers' wives not only had to do the usual housekeeping and food preparation, but also schooling of any children in residence.

The first keeper William Prior made the 24-mile walk to Marquette to visit his dying sister. After her funeral he walked back to the lighthouse, to find that the assistant keeper did not fulfill his duties, after firing him and a couple more assistant keepers, Prior hired his son George to be the assistant keeper. Just over a year after he was hired, he fell on the steps of the landing crib. Keeper Prior took him to the hospital in Marquette on April 18, 1901, where his son passed away roughly two months later on June 13. His son's death drove him into a deep depression, and on June 28, he disappeared into the woods with his gun and some strychnine. It was feared that he had gone off to kill himself. A search party was sent out, but they were not able to find him.

Over a year later, the following entry was made in the station log:

> *Mr. Fred Babcock came to the station 12:30 pm. While hunting in the woods one and a half mile south of the station this noon he found a skeleton of a man hanging to a tree. We went to the place with him and found that the clothing and everything tally with the former keeper of this station who has been missing for seventeen months.*

By 1941, the light was automated, and between 1951 – 1952, the building and land were leased to the U.S. Army. Soldiers were stationed at the lighthouse for two-week periods of anti-aircraft artillery training. Large guns were placed on the cliff, and targets were towed by planes over Lake Superior for practice. The soldiers lived in the meadow and woods to the west of the beacon. One of the soldiers stationed at the lighthouse murdered the owner of the Lumberjack Tavern in the town of Big Bay for raping his wife. The book and movie *Anatomy Of A Murder* are based on this crime.

In 1961, the lighthouse and it's surrounding property were sold to a private owner. Today, it is the only operational lighthouse with a bed and breakfast. Rumor is the ghost of keeper Prior still haunts the old lighthouse. I am not sure if the rumor is true, but I do know it is a beautiful lighthouse, and would be nice place to stay at. You can check out their website http://bigbaylighthouse.com/

Trip Tip: Alder Falls is a few miles south east of Big Bay and is a beautiful waterfall but is difficult to find and access. The waterfall is in a steep gorge, and if you are up to a somewhat challenging hike, it is worth the climb. The water fall is on a two-track off M-550, and on Google maps its marked as Alder Falls Truck Trail, but there is no sign on M-550. last time I was there, in 2008, a small wooden sign on the truck trail marked the trail to the falls.

The Old Upper Peninsula Brewing Company

Location: 105 Meeske Avenue, Marquette, MI 49855

A few miles south of downtown Marquette visible from US-41, is a small stone building with battlements which are notches along the roof like you would see on the top a a castle. The building is known as the Charles Meeske House on the National Register of Historic Places, and was also part of the Upper Peninsula Brewing Co. The structure served as the home and office of brewer Charles Meeske, secretary-treasurer and later president of the company. The building originally had a tunnel leading to the brewery, allowing Meeske to ignore a strange state law prohibiting a person from entering a brewery after sundown. I tried to find a reference to this law, but I was not able to find one although there were some strange laws passed before and including prohibition.

The Upper Peninsula Brewing Company was started in 1849 by German immigrant George Rublein who supplied beer to the thirsty Yoopers of Michigan. In the 1890s, Charles Meeske was the brewery's treasurer. He and the president of the brewery, Reiner Hoch, purchased the company, and under their leadership, the brewery thrived. Meeske built a bottling complex out of sandstone that looked like a castle. In 1895, the business had a production capacity of 25,000 barrels a year. The name of the beer was Drei Kaiser, which means "Three Kings" in German. With the breakout of World War I, the name was changed to Castle Brew.

Marquette County passed a prohibition ordinance in 1916, four years before the United States Government outlawed the sale and manufacturing of alcohol. Because of the ban on liquor, the bottling plant closed and never reopened after prohibition was repealed in 1933. The old castle-like brewery and bottling plants were demolished in the 70s, and the little stone house and office building was the only part of the business left standing. In 1982 the little castle home near Marquette was restored and the building is currently home to the Marquette law firm of Pence & Numinen, P.C.

Mystery at Sand Point Lighthouse

Location: 16 Water Plant Road, Escanaba, MI 49829

The beautifully restored Sand Point Lighthouse at the northern end of Ludington Park in Escanaba marks the entrance for Little Bay De Noc. The strange thing about this lighthouse is that the tower faces away from the water, as if it were built backwards. In 1867, John Terry was appointed as the first lighthouse keeper during its construction. In 1868, he became ill and died before the dwelling was completed and his wife Mary Terry was appointed to the position of Head Lightkeeper. Because of her husband's tragic death, she was one of the first female lighthouse keepers on the Great Lakes. It was Mary who lit the Fresnel lens in the tower of the lighthouse for the first time on May 13, 1868.

Mary and her late husband John did not have any children, and Mary lived alone in the lighthouse. She proudly fulfilled her duty as lightkeeper for several years until one winter night in 1886 when a fire broke out in the lighthouse taking her life. The Lighthouse was severely damaged and no one knows what started the blaze. The rear door was forced opened, and Mary was found on the floor in the oil- room, where fuel and supplies are stored for the lantern, instead of in bed, where she should have been sleeping, leaving some to speculate foul play was involved. Many people in the town of Escanaba know Mary was careful and diligent in her duties of maintaining the lighthouse, and believed she was robbed and that the fire was set to destroy the evidence. I guess we will never know what happened to Mary or why the lighthouse was seemingly built "backwards," but it is a picturesque lighthouse to visit in Ludington Park.

Trip Tip: The old Chicago fireboat *Joseph Medill* is abandoned and sitting on land a few blocks away from the lighthouse and can be seen on 1st Ave. and North 6th Street.

Bond Falls

Location: 1300 US-41 South, Paulding, MI 49912

Bond Falls are probably the most popular waterfalls on the west side of the Upper Peninsula. The scenic site has been recently updated with a new parking lot and boardwalks that allow for easy access to a breathtaking view. A dam farther up stream controls the flow of the Ontonagon

River on which the falls reside. There are three viewing platforms that have a spectacular view of the falls and are an excellent opportunity to get a perfect photo. Bond Falls is a state scenic site managed by the DNR and a pass is required for entry. If you have a recreation passport on your license plates you are already approved for entry; if not, there is a place to pay for a day pass that is on the honor system. While I was visiting, the DNR was there checking to see if everyone was honest, so be sure to pay for a pass if you don't have one.

Photo Tip: Cloudy days provide the perfect condition to take photos of waterfalls; Lighting is more consistent and darker for a slower shutter speed to get that smooth flowing water look.

Iron County Courthouse

Location: US-2 S. 6th Street, Crystal Falls, MI 49920

A few years ago, I was heading west on M-69 in the Upper Peninsula, and I came around the bend and saw the city of Crystal Falls for the first time. I was awestruck by the sight of the imposing courthouse at the top of the hill overlooking the city. The Richardsonian Romanesque Style building was completed in 1891 and constructed using stone quarried from the nearby Paint River.

The town was named for the crystal clear water cascading over the falls on the nearby Paint River. The city was founded in 1880 and was part of Marquette County. After Iron County was organized in 1885, Crystal Falls became the county seat.

The view from the top of the hill where the courthouse stands is spectacular, and during Autumn's peak color, it's breathtaking.

Michi Fact: The first roadside park in the United States was established in Iron County on what is now US-2.

Portage Lake Lift Bridge

Location: Between Houghton and Hancock in the Keweenaw Peninsula

The most famous bridge in Michigan is the Mackinac Bridge that connects the Upper Peninsula with the Lower Peninsula and it is one of the worlds longest suspension bridges. It was opened to traffic on November 1, 1957. Way up in the Keweenaw Peninsula is another world record bridge. The Portage Lake Lift Bridge connects the cities of

Hancock and Houghton, spanning across Portage Lake. The bridge is the world's heaviest and widest double-decked vertical-lift bridge. It was constructed in 1959 with two road decks and the bottom deck having railroad tracks integrated into the road surface. Vehicle traffic would cross the bridge on the upper deck and trains would cross on the lower deck. The bridge could be raised so that vehicles could cross using the lower deck allowing for boats to pass underneath; and if a train needed to cross the bridge, it would be lowered to connect the lower span. The massive bridge deck could also be raised 100 feet to allow for ships and sailboats to pass under it.

After 1982, trains no longer traveled to the tip of the Keweenaw Peninsula and so the bridge is left in the middle position during the summer. After the lake freezes in the cold Michigan winter the bridge is lowered to its bottom position to allow snowmobilers to use the lower span to cross between cites.

It's hard to miss this massive iron giant with its twin towers looking over Houghton and Hancock. After the sun sets, it is a majestic site to see it illuminated like a monument to mankind's engineering achievements.

The Italian Hall disaster

Location: 400 block of 7th Street, on the corner of 7th and Elm, Calumet, MI 49913

I wish this was a story about a wonderful Christmas miracle, but instead, it's about a celebration that ended in tragedy.

The town of Calumet in the Keweenaw Peninsula was one of the wealthiest towns in the United States in the late 1800s because of its copper deposits and mining industry. On Christmas Eve in 1913, after being on strike for five months, copper miners and their families gathered for a yuletide party on the second floor of the Italian Hall in Calumet. During the party for the striking miners, someone yelled, "Fire!" Although there was no fire, seventy-three people died while attempting to escape down a stairwell.

Over half of those who died were children between the ages of six and ten. The belief is that the door at the bottom of the stairway opened inward, and other sources say it opened outward toward the streets, but the narrow stairway became congested and after the first person fell, it became a "domino effect" with people being trampled trying to escape what they thought was a fire. The tragic event was part of the reason building codes were enacted for building capacity and fire escapes. The perpetrator who yelled "FIRE" creating the tragedy was never identified. Some historians believe that "fire" was called out by an anti-union ally of mine management to disrupt the party. The event was memorialized by Woody Guthrie in the song "1913 Massacre", which claims the doors were held shut on the outside by "the copper boss's thug men."

The Italian Hall was built in 1908 as headquarters for Calumet's Benevolent Society. The Society, organized along ethnic lines, encouraged and financially aided immigrants and provided relief to victims of hardship. Following the 1913 Christmas Eve tragedy, the hall continued to be used for nearly five decades. The two-story red brick building was razed in 1984, but the doorway with its stone arch was left standing as a memorial to the people who lost their lives in the 1913 disaster.

Lake Linden City Hall and the Propeller

Location: 401 South Calumet Street, Lake Linden, MI 49945

Near Calumet in the Keweenaw Peninsula is the town of Lake Linden. It sits along the shores of Torch Lake but the town was named after the linden trees that grew along the shoreline. In the center of town is a magnificent city hall building that proudly serves the citizens of Lake Linden. A new hall was needed after a devastating fire in 1887 that wiped out most of the town. The old city hall

148

survived, but the city leaders authorized the construction of a new fire-resistant brick city hall in 1901. The hall also contained a fire station to protect the town from another destructive fire. The most peculiar thing about the city hall is an old bent up propeller that is proudly displayed in front the building.

The propeller is from the *Lady Be Good*, an American B-24 Liberator that went missing in April of 1943. The airplane with its nine man crew went missing on a bombing raid in Naples. The army believed the plane crashed in the Mediterranean Sea since no trace of the airplane was ever found.

In 1958, an oil exploration team from British Petroleum found the remains of the old WWII bomber in the Libyan Desert 440 miles inland. Investigators believed that during a sandstorm the airplane flew past the air base where they were supposed to land. After the sandstorm subsided they saw the moonlight reflecting off the wavy sands of the desert and believed they were still over the water and continued flying. The crew bailed out of the Liberator when they used up all the fuel. The remains of eight of the crewmen were found 100 miles away from the crash site.

Among the remains recovered was Sgt. Robert E. LaMotte from Lake Linden who was the radio operator of the ill-fated flight. The propeller was placed in front of the hall as a memorial in honor of the crew of the *Lady Be Good*.

Continental Fire Company

Location: 408 East Montezuma Avenue, Houghton, MI 49931

I see an old historic fire station, and I think back to the days of firefighters racing out of the station with a horse drawn steam engine. The fire house was a vital part of the community, and in the case of the old fire station in Houghton, it was the beginning one of Michigan's well-respected universities.

The Continental Fire Company was organized in 1860 and is one of the oldest volunteer fire departments in the Upper Peninsula. In 1883, they built an new fire hall in downtown Houghton to house the horses and fire engines. The second floor of the newly constructed building was used as offices by the village. Congressman and Judge Jay Abel Hubbell convinced the Michigan legislature to establish a mining school to train engineers. In 1885, the Michigan Mining School was established, and Hubbell donated land for the school's buildings. Because it was a new school and did not have any buildings, the four teachers and 23 students held their first classes on the second floor of the fire hall. The Michigan Mining School, which eventually became Michigan Technological University, used the fire hall from 1886 to 1889.

As the city of Houghton expanded, it eventually outgrew the second floor of the old fire hall and moved out in the 1930s. To accommodate the larger fire trucks, the city built a new fire station in 1974. The grand old fire hall that served the community for almost a century was listed as a Michigan State Historic Site in 1976. A few years later, the university that was started in the old building purchased it in 1978. It was mainly used for storage by Michigan Tech.

The University sold the building in 2010 to a private group and is currently used as a nightclub.

Quincy Dredge Number 2

Location: North of Houghton and Hancock on M-26

If you are traveling through the Keweenaw Peninsula on M-26 you will come across this giant metal monster, rusting away on the shoreline of Torch Lake. This is one of those places you have to visit and see for yourself. A photograph can't convey the enormous size of the dredge.

After copper was discovered in the Keweenaw Peninsula, many mining operations began to extract the valuable metal from the ore mined in the region. Stamping mills were built to crush the ore and separate the copper. The ore that was pounded down to sand was washed out into a nearby lake or river. The Quincy Mining Company Stamp Mill built in 1888 near Torch Lake (the one in the Keweenaw Peninsula not the one near Traverse City) was one of several stamp mills in the area, and as the mills became more efficient, the sand in the lake was reclaimed and reprocessed to extract the copper that was missed in earlier processing. The Calumet and Hecla Mining Company had the dredge built in 1914 to retrieve the sand from Torch Lake for their mill in the city of Lake Linden. In 1951, the Quincy Mining Company purchased the dredge and named it Quincy Dredge Number Two since they already owned another dredge. During the winter layup in 1967, the dredge sank and with the company struggling to make a profit, they just left it where it sank and it still sits there to this day. In 1978, the state declared it an historic site.

Trip Tip: The Quincy Mining Company Stamp Mills Historic District, with the remains of Stamp Mill Number One, are across the street from where the abandoned dredge rests.

Bibliography

Ste Ann's De'Detroit Church.newworldencyclopedia.org/entry/Michigan
http://www.ste-anne.org/

https://en.wikipedia.org/wiki/Ste._Anne_de_Detroit_Catholic_Church

https://en.wikipedia.org/wiki/Gabriel_Richard

Twin Towers

http://www.mlive.com/news/jackson/index.ssf/2013/05/peek_through_time_irish_h
ills.html

http://www.lenconnect.com/article/20120727/NEWS/307279910

https://en.wikipedia.org/wiki/Irish_Hills_Towers

http://sometimes-interesting.com/2016/03/14/revenant-of-the-irish-hills-towers/

https://www.facebook.com/irishhillstowers/

http://www.freep.com/story/news/local/michigan/2015/11/17/irish-hills-towers-
renovation/75956084/

James Scott Castle

http://detroit1701.org/JamesScottMansion.html

http://www.crainsdetroit.com/article/20160405/BLOG016/160409917/joel-landy-
begins-rebuild-of-james-scotts-spite-house

http://www.mlive.com/business/detroit/index.ssf/2016/03/27_apartments_planned_
for_18-m.html

St. Joseph Pier-head Lighthouse

http://www.stjoelighthouse.com/history-of-st-joseph/

http://www.lighthousefriends.com/light.asp?ID=186

https://en.wikipedia.org/wiki/St._Joseph,_Michigan

http://www.terrypepper.com/lights/michigan/stjoseph/stjoseph.htm

https://www.uscg.mil/history/weblighthouses/lhmi.asp

The Haunted Eloise Asylum

https://en.wikipedia.org/wiki/Eloise_(psychiatric_hospital)

http://www.clickondetroit.com/features/michigans-most-haunted-eloise-psychiatric-hospital

http://www.mlive.com/news/detroit/index.ssf/2015/12/volunteers_work_to_reveal_myst.html

http://www.freep.com/story/news/local/michigan/wayne/2015/11/09/eloise-complex-mental-hospital/75445276/

Climax Post Office and R.F.D.

Roming, Walter (1986) *Michigan Place Names*. Wayne State University Press

https://en.wikipedia.org/wiki/Rural_Free_Delivery

https://en.wikipedia.org/wiki/Climax_Post_Office_Building

http://postalmuseumblog.si.edu/rural-free-delivery/

Hecker Castle on Woodward

https://en.wikipedia.org/wiki/Frank_J._Hecker

https://www.nps.gov/nr/travel/detroit/d29.htm

https://en.wikipedia.org/wiki/Col._Frank_J._Hecker_House

Eckert, K. B. (1993). *Buildings of Michigan*. New York: Oxford University Press.

Genat, Robert (2010). *Woodward Avenue: Cruising the Legendary Strip*. North Branch, MN: CarTech Books.

https://en.wikipedia.org/wiki/M-1_(Michigan_highway)

https://www.michigan.gov/documents/MDOT_Woodward_Heart_and_Soul_170072_7.pdf

The Historic Ypsilanti Water Tower

Roming, Walter (1986) *Michigan Place Names*. Wayne State University Press

http://cityofypsilanti.com/325/Ypsilanti-History

https://en.wikipedia.org/wiki/Ypsilanti,_Michigan

https://en.wikipedia.org/wiki/Ypsilanti_Water_Tower

http://www.michmarkers.com/detail.asp?txtID=S0642

Old State Prison in Jackson

https://en.wikipedia.org/wiki/Michigan_State_Prison

http://www.experiencejackson.com/things-to-do/tours/historic-prison-tour

http://www.mlive.com/living/jackson/index.ssf/2010/12/peek_through_time_jackson_pris.html

http://historicprisontours.com/

The Heart of Rock and Roll in Kalamazoo

http://heritageguitar.com/history/

https://en.wikipedia.org/wiki/Gibson_Guitar_Corporation

http://www.mlive.com/news/kalamazoo/index.ssf/2015/03/gibson_kalamazoo_and_a_guitar.html#0

http://www.mlive.com/news/kalamazoo/index.ssf/2017/01/renovation_of_heritage_guitar.html

Downtown Ann Arbor

Roming, Walter (1986) *Michigan Place Names*. Wayne State University Press

Felt Mansion

Godfrey, L. S., Sceurman, M., & Moran, M. (2006). *Weird Michigan: your travel guide to Michigan's local legends and best kept secrets.* New York: Sterling Publishing.

http://www.feltmansion.org/

https://en.wikipedia.org/wiki/Dorr_E._Felt_Mansion

http://michigansotherside.com/haunted-felt-mansion/

https://en.wikipedia.org/wiki/Dorr_Felt

Livingstone Memorial Light

http://www.lighthousefriends.com/light.asp?ID=163

http://detroit1701.org/Livingstone%20Lighthouse.html

http://lighthouse.boatnerd.com/gallery/detroit/LivingstonMem.htm

https://www.uscg.mil/history/weblighthouses/lhmi.asp

Rattle Run Church Murder

Naldrett, A. (2015). *Lost towns of eastern Michigan.* Charleston, SC: The History Press.

Roming, Walter (1986) *Michigan Place Names.* Wayne State University Press

http://archives.chicagotribune.com/1909/01/12/page/1/article/evil-eye-caused-preacher-to-slay

https://cdnc.ucr.edu/cgi-bin/cdnc?a=d&d=SFC19090112.2.89

Curwood Castle

http://www.sdl.lib.mi.us/history/curwood.html

https://en.wikipedia.org/wiki/James_Oliver_Curwood

http://www.shiawasseehistory.com/curwood.html

https://en.wikipedia.org/wiki/Curwood_Castle

http://www.michigan.org/property/curwood-castle-museum

Bruce Mansion

http://www.clickondetroit.com/community/michigan-mansion-built-in-1876-full-of-architecture-history

http://www.mihaunted.com/

http://www.brucemansion.com/

Roming, Walter (1986) *Michigan Place Names*. Wayne State University Press

House Of Seven Gables

Eckert, K. B. (1993). *Buildings of Michigan*. New York: Oxford University Press.

http://www.huroncitymuseums.org/

http://www.michmarkers.com/startup.asp?startpage=L0463.htm

http://www.michigansthumb.com/news/article/Huron-City-Museums-event-set-for-Saturday-7322729.php

Hells Half Mile

http://bay-journal.com/bay/1he/writings/lumbering-town-blazed-trail.html

http://www.nailhed.com/2014/04/alternative-history-bay-city-pt-2.html

Hoskins, Lisa (2009) *Ghosts of Bay City, Saginaw, and Midland* Schiffer Publishing Limited

Barber, S. (2012). *Myths and mysteries of Michigan: true stories of the unsolved and unexplained*. Guilford, CT: Globe Pequot Press.

White, Edward (1907) *The Blazed Trail*

The Death of the Sparling men in Tyre

Howard, J. (2008). *The thumb pointed fingers*. Staunton, VA: Lot's Wife Pub.

Roming, Walter (1986) *Michigan Place Names*. Wayne State University Press

http://murderpedia.org/male.M/m/macgregor-robert.htm

https://greatlakesbaymag.com/first-harm/

The Cat Lady House in Saginaw

http://media.mlive.com/saginawnews_impact/other/DeGesero%20House.pdf

http://www.mlive.com/news/saginaw/index.ssf/2016/04/saginaw_to_demolish_hist oric_l.html

https://www.facebook.com/SaveRosemarysTheCatLadysHouse/

White Rock Lighthouse

Roming, Walter (1986) *Michigan Place Names.* Wayne State University Press

https://review-mag.com/article/neglected-treasures-the-fight-to-preserve-a-rare-lumber-baron-mansion-with-a-rich-significant-history

http://www.ipl.org/div/light/GL/WhiteRock.html

https://stacynelliott.wordpress.com/2012/04/30/spotlight-on-a-small-town-white-rock/

https://en.wikipedia.org/wiki/Treaty_of_Detroit

http://www.kansasheritage.org/PBP/books/treaties/t_1807.html

Mt Pleasant Industrial Boarding School

http://www.themorningsun.com/article/MS/20160606/NEWS/160609800

http://www.sagchip.org/news.aspx?newsid=6#.WOJaXlXyuUk

http://www.sagchip.org/ziibiwing/planyourvisit/boardingschool/index2.htm

http://www.michigan.gov/documents/mshda/mshda_shpo_20161221_nr_indian_in dustrial_546574_7.pdf

https://en.wikipedia.org/wiki/Mount_Pleasant_Indian_Industrial_Boarding_School

Santa House In Midland

http://www.midlandfoundation.org/santa-house/

http://www.midlandfoundation.org/news/2012/11/26/history-of-midlands-santa-house.html

http://www.ourmidland.com/news/article/Midland-Santa-House-opens-6960101.php

http://www.mlive.com/midland/index.ssf/2012/11/santa_claus_is_coming_to_main_street_to_light_up_the_town_see_his_revamped_house_in_midland.html

Saginaw River Rear Range Lighthouse

https://www.uscg.mil/history/weblighthouses/lhmi.asp

http://www.lighthousefriends.com/light.asp?ID=173

https://en.wikipedia.org/wiki/Saginaw_River_Rear_Range_Light

http://www.saginawriver.com/

http://www.coastalliving.com/travel/top-15-haunted-lighthouses/haunted-lighthouses-saginaw-river-lighthouse

http://www.mybaycity.com/scripts/p3_v2/P3V3-0200.cfm?P3_ArticleID=8068

Oleszewski, W. (1998). *Great Lakes lighthouses, American & Canadian: a comprehensive directory/guide to Great Lakes lighthouses, American & Canadian.* Gwinn, MI: Avery Color Studios.

Ladies of the Maccabees Building in Port Huron

http://www.phoenixmasonry.org/masonicmuseum/fraternalism/maccabees.htm

https://en.wikipedia.org/wiki/Knights_of_the_Maccabees

Eckert, K. B. (1993). *Buildings of Michigan.* New York: Oxford University Press.

http://www.historyswomen.com/socialreformer/binawest.html

https://www.findagrave.com/cgi-bin/fg.cgi?page=gr&GRid=95156884

Alonzo Hart Murder

http://www.themorningsun.com/article/MS/20160219/NEWS/160219650

http://www.theoaklandpress.com/article/OP/20160219/NEWS/160219382

http://www.mlive.com/news/saginaw/index.ssf/2008/04/parole board_will_consider_rel.html

https://www.findagrave.com/cgi-bin/fg.cgi?page=gr&GRid=65408386

Hoyt Library

http://www.saginaw.lib.mi.us/hoyt.html

https://en.wikipedia.org/wiki/Hoyt_Library

http://www.michmarkers.com/detail.asp?txtID=L2040

http://www.hauntedsaginaw.com/

http://www.mlive.com/entertainment/saginaw/index.ssf/2015/11/a_haunting_at_hoyt_library_bri.html

The Two Story Outhouse

Godfrey, L. S., Sceurman, M., & Moran, M. (2006). *Weird Michigan: your travel guide to Michigan's local legends and best kept secrets*. New York: Sterling Publishing.

http://www.roadsideamerica.com/tip/657

https://en.wikipedia.org/wiki/Home_Township,_Montcalm_County,_Michigan

http://www.topix.com/forum/city/cedar-lake-mi/TSM56M7LIPAQA04FS

The Brick Flag of Little Michigan

http://www.michigan-sportsman.com/forum/threads/stupid-question.269083/

The Ghost Town of Melbourne

Roming, Walter (1986) *Michigan Place Names*. Wayne State University Press

That Centennial Passing Over Old Melbourne 1954 Valley Tales. The Saginaw News

LaMat, James (1967) *Burt's Town Of Melbourne Erased by Mysterious Fire in 1876* . The Saginaw News

Manistee Fire Station

http://www.manisteemi.gov/129/Fire-EMS

http://www.manisteemi.gov/DocumentCenter/View/2302

http://www.michmarkers.com/Pages/L1647.htm

http://www.michigan.org/property/manistee-city-fire-station

Grousehaven Lodge

https://en.wikipedia.org/wiki/Rifle_River_State_Recreation_Area

https://www.michigan.gov/documents/dnr/RIFLE_RIVER_GENERAL_MANAG EMENT_PLAN_V.5.15.2007APPROVED_PLAN_298453_7.pdf

https://www.hemmings.com/magazine/hcc/2008/08/Harry-Jewett/1675840.html

http://rosecity-mi.us/purple-gang/

Five Channels Dam

http://www.michmarkers.com/startup.asp?startpage=L2143.htm

https://en.wikipedia.org/wiki/Five_Channels_Dam

http://www.mlive.com/business/jackson-lansing/index.ssf/2012/12/consumers_energy_unveils_portr.html

https://en.wikipedia.org/wiki/Hydroelectric_power_in_the_United_States

https://energy.gov/eere/water/history-hydropower

Tawas Point Lighthouses

https://www.uscg.mil/history/weblighthouses/lhmi.asp

http://www.lighthousefriends.com/light.asp?ID=175

http://www.terrypepper.com/lights/huron/tawas/tawas.htm

Oleszewski, W. (1998). *Great Lakes lighthouses, American & Canadian: a comprehensive directory/guide to Great Lakes lighthouses, American & Canadian.* Gwinn, MI: Avery Color Studios.

Our Lady Of The Woods Shrine in Mio

http://ourladyofthewoodsshrine.org/

https://www.facebook.com/pages/Our-Lady-Of-The-Woods-Shrine

http://www.dioceseofgaylord.org/member-813/st.-mary-our-lady-of-the-woods-shrine-152.html

http://www.michigan.org/property/our-lady-woods-shrine

Woolsey Memorial Airport

http://www.record-eagle.com/archives/cute-airport-tragic-story-woolsey-a-hero/article_289b7410-04f7-53d2-8f00-8c021b01fa01.html

https://www.findagrave.com/cgi-bin/fg.cgi?page=gr&GRid=14848276

http://www.leelanaunews.com/news/2015-07-02/Life_in_Leelanau/Woolsey_Airport_hits_80th_birthday_heres_how_the_f.html

https://www.facebook.com/WoolseyMemorialAirport

Rolling Up Hill Near Rose City

https://en.wikipedia.org/wiki/List_of_gravity_hills

The Alden Train Depot

http://www.michmarkers.com/startup.asp?startpage=L1429.htm

http://www.visitalden.com/historyofalden/depotmuseumhistsite.html

Roming, Walter (1986) *Michigan Place Names.* Wayne State University Press

The Old Petoskey Library

http://www.petoskeylibrary.org/about-the-library/history-of-the-library/

https://en.wikipedia.org/wiki/List_of_Carnegie_libraries_in_Michigan

https://www.northernexpress.com/news/feature/article-7292-legacy-of-learning/

Ocqueoc Falls

http://www.michigan.gov/dnr/0,4570,7-153-10366_41825-283510--,00.html

http://www.us23heritageroute.org/cheboygan.asp?ait=av&aid=331

Wreck Of The Joseph S. Fay

http://www.40milepointlighthouse.org/fay.html

http://thunderbay.noaa.gov/shipwrecks/fay.html

https://en.wikipedia.org/wiki/Forty_Mile_Point_Light

http://www.us23heritageroute.org/location.asp?ait=av&aid=4292

Seven Bridges Recreation Area

https://www.gtrlc.org/recreation-events/preserve/seven-bridges/

http://mynorth.com/2012/11/tribute-to-former-michigan-first-lady-helen-milliken/

http://www.upnorthtrails.org/trails/seven-bridges.html

https://www.michigan.gov/documents/dnr/Cmpt171_Sum7BridgesMgtPlan_217515_7.pdf

Middle Village

http://www.visitharborspringsmichigan.com/stories/st_ignatius_church_middle_villa ge

http://www.michiganwatertrails.org/location.asp?ait=av&aid=699

http://www.michmarkers.com/startup.asp?startpage=L0491.htm

Roming, Walter (1986) *Michigan Place Names.* Wayne State University Press

Lost In Michigan

Cheboygan Lighthouse Ruins

https://michpics.wordpress.com/2013/01/05/the-ruins-of-the-cheboygan-point-lighthouse/

http://www.lighthousefriends.com/light.asp?ID=218

http://www.terrypepper.com/lights/huron/cheboygan-main/

McGulpin Point Lighthouse

http://www.mcgulpinpoint.org/

https://en.wikipedia.org/wiki/McGulpin_Point_Light

http://www.emmetcounty.org/parks-recreation/mcgulpin-point-lighthouse/

http://www.terrypepper.com/lights/michigan/mcgulpin/index.html

Oleszewski, W. (1998). *Great Lakes lighthouses, American & Canadian: a comprehensive directory/guide to Great Lakes lighthouses, American & Canadian.* Gwinn, MI: Avery Color Studios.

Fort Mackinac Post Cemetery

https://www.cem.va.gov/cems/lots/fort_mackinac.asp

http://www.mightymac.org/fortmackinacemetery.htm

https://www.findagrave.com/cgi-bin/fg.cgi?page=cr&CRid=1985420

The Haunted Ghost Town of Shelldrake

Roming, Walter (1986) *Michigan Place Names.* Wayne State University Press

https://en.wikipedia.org/wiki/Shelldrake,_Michigan

http://www.prairieghosts.com/sheldrak.html

Godfrey, Linda S., Mark Sceurman, and Mark Moran. Weird Michigan: Your Travel Guide to Michigan's Local Legends and Best Kept Secrets. New York: Sterling, 2006. Print.

http://www.michmarkers.com/

165

King of the File Folder's Mackinac Island Cottage

Porter, P. (2006). *View from the veranda: the history and architecture of the summer cottages on Mackinac Island.* Mackinac Island, MI: Mackinac Island State Park Commission.

Kitter, W. (2015). *A place that I love: a tour drivers perspective of Mackinac Island.* United States: Xlibris.

http://www.mackinacislandnews.com/news/2010-08-21/Columnists/Amberg_Family_Mother_Cabrini_Provide_Help_to_Itali.html

Luce County Sheriff's House and Jail

https://en.wikipedia.org/wiki/Luce_County_Sheriff%27s_House_and_Jail

http://www.exploringthenorth.com/newberry/histmuseum.html

http://www.explorem123.com/points-of-interest/luce-county-historical-museum/

http://www.michmarkers.com/

Roming, Walter (1986) *Michigan Place Names.* Wayne State University Press

Big Bay Point Lighthouse

https://www.bigbaylighthouse.com/

Oleszewski, W. (1998). *Great Lakes lighthouses, American & Canadian: a comprehensive directory/guide to Great Lakes lighthouses, American & Canadian.* Gwinn, MI: Avery Color Studios.

http://www.uscg.mil/history/weblighthouses/lhmi.asp

http://www.lighthousefriends.com/light.asp?ID=574

https://en.wikipedia.org/wiki/Big_Bay_Point_Light

The Old Upper Peninsula Brewing Company

https://en.wikipedia.org/wiki/Upper_Peninsula_Brewing_Company_Building

Eckert, K. B. (1993). *Buildings of Michigan.* New York: Oxford University Press.

Magnaghi, R. M. (2015). *Upper Peninsula beer: a history of brewing above the bridge.* Charleston, SC: American Palate.

Sand Point Lighthouse

http://www.lighthousefriends.com/light.asp?ID=561

http://www.terrypepper.com/lights/michigan/sandpoint/sandpoint.htm

Oleszewski, W. (1998). *Great Lakes lighthouses, American & Canadian: a comprehensive directory/guide to Great Lakes lighthouses, American & Canadian.* Gwinn, MI: Avery Color Studios.

Bond Falls

http://www.michigan.org/property/bond-falls-scenic-site

https://en.wikipedia.org/wiki/Bond_Falls

http://www.gowaterfalling.com/waterfalls/bond.shtml

Iron County Courthouse

Eckert, K. B. (1993). *Buildings of Michigan.* New York: Oxford University Press.

Roming, Walter (1986) *Michigan Place Names.* Wayne State University Press

https://ironmi.org/departments/courthouse/

Portage Lake Lift Bridge

https://en.wikipedia.org/wiki/Portage_Lake_Lift_Bridge

http://www.michigan.gov/mdot/0,4616,7-151-9623_11154_11188-28585--,00.html

http://historicbridges.org/bridges/browser/?bridgebrowser=michigan/houghtonhancock/

The Italian Hall disaster

https://en.wikipedia.org/wiki/Italian_Hall_disaster

http://www.huffingtonpost.com/steve-lehto/the-italian-hall-disaster_b_1120771.html

http://michigansotherside.com/the-tragedy-at-italian-hall/

Lehto, S. (2013). *Deaths door: the truth behind the Italian Hall disaster and the strike of 1913.* Royal Oak, MI: Momentum Books, L.L.C.

Lake Linden City Hall and the Propeller

https://en.wikipedia.org/wiki/Lake_Linden_Village_Hall_and_Fire_Station

Eckert, K. B. (1993). *Buildings of Michigan.* New York: Oxford University Press.

Roming, Walter (1986) *Michigan Place Names.* Wayne State University Press

https://en.wikipedia.org/wiki/Lady_Be_Good_(aircraft)

http://www.ladybegood.net/

Continental Fire Company

https://en.wikipedia.org/wiki/Houghton_Fire_Hall

http://www.mtu.edu/stratplan/history/

http://www.secondwavemedia.com/upper-peninsula/devnews/Continental2222012.aspx

https://en.wikipedia.org/wiki/Michigan_Technological_University

http://www.mtu.edu/magazine/spring10/stories/archives/

Quincy Dredge no. 2

https://en.wikipedia.org/wiki/Quincy_Dredge_Number_Two

http://www.coppercountryexplorer.com/2009/02/the-mining-of-torch-lake/

http://www.ship-wreck.com/shipwreck/keweenaw/dredge.html

I hope you will continue
to follow my journey at
www.LostInMichigan.net

Made in the USA
Middletown, DE
27 January 2023